CATHOLIC IDEAS FOR A SECULAR WORLD

O. Carter Snead, *series editor*

The purpose of this interdisciplinary series is to feature authors from around the world who will expand the influence of Catholic thought on the most important conversations in academia and the public square. The series is "Catholic" in the sense that the books will emphasize and engage the enduring themes of human dignity and flourishing, the common good, truth, beauty, justice, and freedom in ways that reflect and deepen principles affirmed by the Catholic Church for millennia. It is not limited to Catholic authors or even works that explicitly take Catholic principles as a point of departure. Its books are intended to demonstrate the diversity and enhance the relevance of these enduring themes and principles in numerous subjects, ranging from the arts and humanities to the sciences.

Not
by Nature
but
by Grace

Forming Families through Adoption

GILBERT C. MEILAENDER

University of Notre Dame Press

Notre Dame, Indiana

Published by the University of Notre Dame Press
Notre Dame, Indiana 46556
www.undpress.nd.edu
Copyright © 2016 by the University of Notre Dame

Manufactured in the United States of America

Library of Congress Cataloging-in-Publication Data

Names: Meilaender, Gilbert, 1946– author.

Title: Not by nature but by grace : forming families through adoption / Gilbert C. Meilaender.

Description: Notre Dame : University of Notre Dame Press, 2016. | Series: Catholic ideas for a secular world | Includes bibliographical references and index. | Description based on print version record and CIP data provided by publisher; resource not viewed.

Identifiers: LCCN 2016020343 (print) | LCCN 2016019555 (ebook) | ISBN 9780268100704 (pdf) | ISBN 9780268100711 (epub) | ISBN 9780268100681 (hardcover : alk. paper)

Subjects: LCSH: Families—Religious aspects—Christianity. | Adoption (Theology) | Adoption—Religious aspects—Christianity.

Classification: LCC BT707.7 (print) | LCC BT707.7 .M45 2016 (ebook) | DDC 261.8/35874—dc23

LC record available at https://lccn.loc.gov/2016020343

∞*This paper meets the requirements of ANSI/NISO Z39.48-1992 (Permanence of Paper).*

To Peter and Derek, brothers,

and

To Nicolas, Nathanael,

and Luke, brothers

Contents

Introduction

The first chapter of Luke's Gospel tells us that on the eighth day after Zechariah and Elizabeth had been blessed in their old age with the gift of a son, they gathered with neighbors and kin for the circumcision and naming of the boy. Those gathered assumed that he should be named Zechariah after his father, but Elizabeth said, "Not so; he shall be called John." But, responded the others, "None of your kindred is called by this name." So they turned to Zechariah, who had been unable to speak since his encounter in the temple with the angel Gabriel. Handed a writing tablet, he wrote, "His name is John."[1]

John, after all, was an unexpected gift of grace to his parents, hardly to be expected by anyone who understood the givens of our natural condition. But John was not born to them simply to continue a line of kinship and descent. Rather, he was to play an essential role in a decisively new historical event, one that far surpassed anything that might seem naturally possible. Perhaps it is no surprise, therefore, that he warned those who came to listen to him not to place their confidence in ties of flesh and blood (thinking themselves secure as descendants of Abraham).[2] Yet, the connection to Abraham remained important; for, as

St. Paul puts it, gentile followers of Jesus were simply branches grafted onto that Abrahamic root.[3]

Nature counts. So does history. Both play important roles in the chapters to come, but it is essential to keep in mind that adoption is a work not of nature but of grace. Within theological ethics the last several centuries have seen an increasing turn to history; indeed, that might be said to be a characteristic emphasis of the modern period. It may be, though, that we can illumine the importance—and the limits—of history at least as much by focusing on a particular question as by developing a theory. That, at any rate, is my aim here.

This little study takes adoption as its focus. I do this, first of all, simply because adoption raises for us questions of great practical importance. But it is also true that directing our attention to adoption is a way of bringing into focus the problem of relating nature and history within Christian faith. Consequently, the chapters that follow may seem, I grant, to be a rather idiosyncratic discussion of adoption. Although I try to pay attention to many of the issues that are regularly part of adoption discussions (especially in chapter 3), the center of my concern is the meaning of adoption for Christian theology. That may help to explain why I devote two chapters to thinking about how best to relate adoption to technologies of assisted reproduction and to what has come to be called embryo adoption. The heart of the matter is that adoption is a work not of nature but of grace.

In the first chapter I use literature, theological reflection, and several religious traditions to think through—and puzzle over—the complicated ways in which nature and history work to form families. The second chapter develops what I take to be the basic Christian understanding of adoption, which, as it happens, is an important concept in the New Testament. I recognize, of course, that the practice of adoption in our society raises a wide range of questions and concerns. Hence, while the heart of my interest is theological, I examine some of these other concerns in chapter 3, offering the best response I can to a number of questions that often puzzle us. The fourth and fifth chapters explore particular questions that arise for people, like us, who live in a world where both adoption and assisted reproduction are common. In their—by my lights, appropriate—concern about many uses of new reproductive technologies, Christians can too easily develop arguments that might almost seem to undermine the legitimacy of adoption. I try in chapter 4 to do justice to their concern without losing the central importance of adoption for Christian thinking. The increasingly widespread use of reproductive technologies has also produced a world in which there are thousands of frozen embryos. Whether we should think of those embryos as suitable candidates for "adoption" is a puzzling question, taken up in chapter 5.

After I had begun to think about this project and read around in the literature about adoption, I realized that these matters had actually been fermenting in my mind for decades. Years ago, when as a much younger man I used to coach boys' baseball teams in the summer, I had a team that practiced on a field adjacent to a home where troubled boys and girls, removed from their homes, lived for a time. When my team practiced, it was not uncommon for boys from the home to come out and engage me in conversation. It didn't matter to them that I was trying to keep order among fifteen or so young boys, that I was trying to pitch batting practice, that I was organizing drills. They would stand out there talking to me and asking me questions.

One day I went home and mentioned to my wife how frustrating this was, how much of my (rather scarce) time they were taking. "You have to remember," she responded, "that you may be the only adult who's really talked politely to them today." I tried to keep that in mind, and I hope I did better at future practices. These were boys who needed a family, a place where they belonged. I was far from providing that, but their eagerness to talk with me was a sign of how much they needed what they did not have and what we did not seem able to provide.

A few years later I published in *The Christian Century* six short letters written to a son whom my wife and I had adopted. But it would be wrong to characterize him as an "adopted son."

He is simply our son, for adoption is not a status that clings to one forever. Hence, the dedication of this book is to two different sets of brothers. In each case one or more is adopted, another is not. But they are simply brothers, as I hope this little book makes clear. Because those letters still seem to me to provide a useful way to think more colloquially about some of this book's themes, I have included four of them as brief interludes between chapters.

I am grateful to two anonymous readers who offered helpful observations and suggestions for the final form of this book. The work of writing it has for the most part taken place under the auspices of the Notre Dame Center for Ethics and Culture. I have enjoyed the congenial support it has provided and am especially grateful to its director, Carter Snead, with whom I have had many helpful discussions about the topics taken up in the pages that follow.

CHAPTER I

Nature and History

Pointing to Sophocles' story of Oedipus as an example of one way in which mythic stories in Western culture have depicted adoption, Marianne Novy writes: "The plot of *Oedipus* is based on the assumption that parenthood is a matter of genetics, which determines identity."[1] To say, as Oedipus does, "I will know who I am," is, Novy notes, "to define your parentage as your identity."[2]

Doing so is, however, by no means as obvious as it might seem. Nature has its claims upon us, but so does history. In a well-ordered world these claims might not seem to be in competition, but, alas, our worlds are often not well ordered. "Critics," Novy reminds us, "almost always refer to Laius and Jocasta as Oedipus's father and mother, without regard to the fact that they both wanted him killed as an infant, or that Jocasta spent only three days with the baby before giving him to the shepherd to expose."[3] To think about the meaning and significance of adoption is to reflect upon lives in which nature and history are not harmoniously ordered. We can consider several puzzling examples as an invitation to engage in such reflection.

In George Eliot's novel *Silas Marner* (published in 1861), a series of tragic events makes Silas—a reclusive weaver without friends or family—the adoptive father for a little orphaned girl whom he names Eppie. Eppie's opium-addicted mother, Molly, dies of exposure on a cold and snowy winter's evening, having been unable to get Godfrey Cass, to whom she was secretly married, to acknowledge his paternity. The little girl wanders into Silas's cottage, he cares for her, and, since her mother is dead and her father unknown, he continues to raise her as his daughter. (There were no children's service agencies to intervene!) When Silas wonders whether he really has a right to the child, Mrs. Winthrop, a kind-hearted neighbor, tells him, "'You'll have a right to her if you're a father to her.'"[4]

Given the circumstances under which Eppie came to him and given the evidence in her hair and eyes that Eppie is not Silas's biological child, it would, of course, be impossible for Silas to pretend that he and his daughter were joined by nature through a biological tie. Nor does he attempt that. As Eppie grows older, Silas shares with her some of the details of how she came to live with him. Eppie puzzles a good bit over her mother, who died in the snow, but she gives relatively little thought to the father she has never known. After all, Eliot writes, "Had she not a father very close to her, who loved her better than real fathers in the village seemed to love their daughters?" (197).

That sentence, simple as it is and ringing true as it does, may nonetheless leave us puzzled. Eppie has a father, indeed a close and loving father, better than other fathers in the village. But Eliot does not just say that. She writes that the love of Eppie's father is better than that of any of the "real" fathers in the village. So in the very sentence that seems to affirm in the strongest terms Silas's fatherhood, those whose tie to their daughters is not just historical but also natural are characterized as real fathers.

It is hard to miss, though, that the story gives Eppie the last word on this puzzle. Her biological father, Godfrey Cass, had experienced Molly's death as liberating. It freed him to marry Nancy Lammeter, a far more respectable choice for a wife than Molly had been. Years pass, Godfrey and Nancy remain childless, and he finally tells Nancy that Eppie is actually his child. Thinking that they are in a position to give Eppie advantages that Silas cannot, they offer to take her into their home and acknowledge her as Godfrey's child.

Eppie resists the idea, wanting to remain with Silas, but Godfrey says: "'I have a claim on you, Eppie—the strongest of all claims. . . . I have a natural claim that must stand before every other'" (228–29). This rouses Silas from his normal reticence, and, pitting history against nature, he replies: "'It's me she's been calling her father ever since she could say the word'" (229). It is Eppie who finally settles the matter, in the following exchange with Nancy:

> "What you say is natural, my dear child—it's natural you should cling to those who've brought you up," she said, mildly; "but there's a duty you owe to your lawful father. There's perhaps something to be given up on more sides than one. When your father opens his home to you, I think it's right you shouldn't turn your back on it."
>
> "I can't feel as I've got any father but one," said Eppie, impetuously, while the tears gathered. (231)

It is hard to imagine most readers of the story not adding their "Amen" to the feeling Eppie expresses, and it is hard to imagine George Eliot not intending that they should. However strong the claims of nature may be, in this story those claims pale into insignificance when set over against the shared familial history of Silas and Eppie. Thus, Marianne Novy writes, *Silas Marner* "makes a case for the benefits and the naturalness of adoption, the redefinition of family by nurture rather than by genetics, more emphatically than any well-known novel before the twentieth century."[5]

How puzzling, then, that Eliot wrote another novel, *Daniel Deronda* (published in 1876), which "makes a powerful case for the view that adoptees must learn their heredity to know who they really are."[6] To attempt to summarize the plot(s) of this mammoth novel is well beyond my critical powers. It is really at least two stories—that of Daniel Deronda and that of Gwendolen Harleth—though the stories intersect in many ways. Critics have sometimes suggested that it would have been better to publish only one of the stories, Gwendolen's or Daniel's, though they do not necessarily agree which it should have been. For my purposes, though, the focus must clearly be on Daniel Deronda.

He is a young English gentleman, who has been raised with love and attention by Sir Hugo Mallinger, whom he calls his uncle. Knowing only that he does not know the identity of his biological father or mother, Daniel cannot help wondering whether Sir Hugo may actually be his father, and he often finds himself longing for a more secure sense of identity and belonging (experiencing, one might say, what some today have taken to calling "genealogical bewilderment").

Through a series of twists and turns rather too fantastic to be entirely believable, Daniel comes to learn that he is Jewish by birth. Having rescued a young Jewish woman named Mirah when she was about to take her own life, Daniel, who is drawn to her more than he perhaps even realizes at first, tries to learn whether her mother or brother is still alive. Although he finds a man who for several reasons might be a plausible candidate for Mirah's brother, this man is a rather unappealing pawnbroker, and Daniel is not certain Mirah would be well served to discover that such a man was her brother. His uncertainties about himself intersect with his concern for Mirah. "How far was he justified in determining another life by his own notions? Was it not his secret complaint against the way in which others had ordered his own life, that he had not open daylight on all its relations, so that he had not, like other men, the full guidance of primary duties?"[7]

Daniel also comes to know a mystical Jewish visionary, Ezra Mordecai Cohen, who is living with the pawnbroker's family. Mordecai is actually Mirah's brother, though it takes some time for Daniel to learn that. In the meantime he comes under Mordecai's spell, becoming something like his disciple. Mordecai is a dying man, and he is looking for someone who will carry forward and work toward his vision of a restored Jewish nation. He sees in Daniel Deronda that someone, and Daniel is not immune to the lure of Mordecai's vision. The problem, of course, is that Daniel is not Jewish. How then could he be the one to carry on the vision of Mordecai?

> "What my birth was does not lie in my will," [Daniel] answered. "My sense of claims on me cannot be independent of my knowledge there. And I cannot promise you that I will try to hasten a disclosure. Feelings which have struck root through half my life may still hinder me from doing what I have never yet been able to do. Everything must be waited for. I must know more of the truth about my own life, and I must know more of what it would become if it were made a part of yours." (2:154–55)

Mordecai is, however, serenely confident that Daniel is in fact Jewish, and events turn out to support his confidence. Deronda's biological mother, Leonora Halm-Eberstein, sends him a letter through Sir Hugo. After having been entirely removed from her child's life for years, she now wants to meet and speak with him. She is Jewish, and her desire to be an opera singer had been opposed by her father and only achieved after his death. For her, being Jewish had been a narrow, restrictive identity against which she had rebelled with all her heart.

Many men had loved her, Sir Hugo among them. But having married her Jewish cousin and given birth to Daniel, she had no desire to raise a child. Moreover, she thought she would be doing her son a favor by releasing him "from the bondage of having been born a Jew" (2:342). "I have not the foolish notion," she says to Daniel, "that you can love me merely because I am your mother, when you have never seen or heard of me all your life. But I thought I chose something better for you than being with me. I did not think that I deprived you of anything worth having" (2:341).

Even though his mother continues to affirm her abandonment of him, there is for Daniel something liberating in learning the truth about his origins. His affection for Sir Hugo remains, but he takes up his Jewish identity eagerly. It frees him to acknowledge his love for Mirah and to see her as a possible wife, something he had not thought possible as long as she was Jewish and he was not. It frees him also to make Mordecai's vision his own. He and Mirah marry and soon leave for the "East," there to devote themselves to the recovery of a Jewish homeland.

Eliot's two novels, taken together, constitute for us a problem. With her identity shaped by their shared history, Eppie feels at home with Silas; living with him as his daughter is where she belongs. Daniel, though loved with much affection by Sir Hugo, always carries about with himself a vague sense of difference, of not belonging. For him that shared history does not overcome a feeling that nature has set him apart. Marianne Novy, acknowledging the contrast, warns that we might make too much of it. After all, Daniel's newfound sense of identity owes at least as much to Mordecai's "spiritual parentage" as to the knowledge Daniel gains from Leonora. Hence, one might still argue that *Daniel Deronda* favors "fostering over kinship."[8]

True as this may be, readers who manage to make their way through the whole of *Daniel Deronda* are likely to think that in weighing the conflicting claims of nature and history it comes down far more on the side of nature as identity-shaping than does *Silas Marner*. Taken together, the novels pose a problem they do not solve.

Consider the contrasting views of two clergymen. Russell Moore is a Southern Baptist theologian, currently serving as president of the Southern Baptist Convention's Ethics and Religious Liberty Commission. He and his wife have five sons, the oldest two of whom were born in Russia, orphaned, and adopted by the Moores. The process of adopting these sons came to have far more than personal significance for Moore; for the experience compelled him to reflect theologically on what it means to be an adopted child or adoptive parent. And his 2009 book, *Adopted for Life: The Priority of Adoption for Christian Families and Churches*, is a powerful and engaging explication of the meaning and significance of adoption.[9]

There is much in his view that we might take up here, much with which to agree and perhaps some with which to disagree. For my purposes at the moment, however, I will concentrate on just one strand of his discussion, his opposition to what might be called biological essentialism. From that standpoint it is "traceable genetic material" that creates the parent-child bond (24). Then adoption becomes simply a second-best, fallback option for couples who experience infertility—"a plan B for people who can't have children" (107).

For Moore, however, adoption seems to be Plan A, though perhaps we should say that he makes this case only with respect to Christians in particular. But Christians, at any rate, are called to recognize as kin, as their own flesh and blood, those with whom they do not share traceable genetic material. A history of relationship, commitment sustained over time, is what forms and sustains the bond of father and mother with their children.

How seriously Moore intends this becomes clear in what seems, to me at least, to be the most striking passage in his book. Recalling that when he and his wife adopted their two sons from Russia, many people encouraged them not to forget to teach these boys about their cultural heritage—meaning by that the heritage of their Russian roots—Moore gives a different spin to that task. "As we see it," he writes, "that's not their heritage anymore, and we hardly want to signal to them that they are strangers and aliens, even welcome ones, in our home. We teach them about their heritage, yes, but their heritage as Mississippians" (36). Thus, the boys learn about their grandfather, a Baptist pastor in the South, their great-grandfather who raised cotton, and the civil rights movement. All this becomes their history.[10]

As far as Moore is concerned, this approach is a natural and necessary outgrowth of Christian faith. The New Testament uses precisely the language of adoption to characterize the manner in which one becomes a Christian—as, for example, in Galatians 4:5, where St. Paul writes that God sent his Son as redeemer "so that we might receive adoption as sons."[11] Hence, adoption creates in believers a new identity, a shared identity. Because it is the means by which one comes to belong to the body of Christ, no one belongs by nature, and all who belong do so by virtue of their adoption. "People will often ask me," Moore writes, "what the key to raising adopted children is. I tell them that honestly, we don't know—we don't have any adopted children. The term 'adopted kid' assumes an ongoing difference, something that differentiates him from a 'regular kid'" (191).

In an essay titled "Adoption after Altruism," Paul Sauer gives voice to a contrasting angle of vision.[12] Sauer is also a clergyman, and he wears several hats—as pastor and executive minister of Our Saviour Lutheran Church and School in the Bronx; as an assistant professor of religion at Concordia College in Bronxville, New York; and as associate editor of the *Lutheran Forum*. More immediately germane to my purpose here is that he, like Moore, is the father of two internationally adopted children. His understanding of the meaning of adoption is rather different from Moore's, however. In part, his view is different simply because he focuses his essay on unethical practices that have sometimes marked international adoptions, even and especially those done under the auspices of "so-called Christian adoption agencies" (12).

More generally, however, he rejects what he calls the "altruistic adoption image," which pictures the adopted child as one who has been rescued from a hopeless, poverty-stricken and abandoned life to something far better. We should not, he says, characterize an adopted child as lucky or fortunate. "A 'lucky child' would be one where there would be no need for adoption because the biological parents . . . would be able to raise the child themselves" (11).[13]

But Sauer is not just troubled by unethical practices. He believes that the "altruistic adoption image" seduces us into overlooking the continuing importance of biological ties in the life of the adopted child. Children adopted from other countries may be left "with little to no sense of their own history" (11). He insists that while, to be sure, "the adoption of children can make them part of an ethnically different family," it remains the case that adoption "does not change their own ethnicity" (12). At least on the face of it, then, the contrast with Russell Moore's approach could hardly be more striking.

This contrast will not disappear, but it is only fair to note that both Moore and Sauer qualify their views in order to acknowledge the complex relation of nature and history in adoption. Sauer sees how understandable it is that would-be adoptive parents should find themselves drawn to the altruistic adoption image. They may quickly come to think that their adoption of a particular child "was meant to be" (12). Moreover, "there will always be a need for adoption" in a world distorted and broken by sin (12). And even after asserting that the adopted child's ethnicity remains what it was, even after noting how important it is that adoptive parents should respect the cultural tradition from which their child came, he writes that such respect means that the parents should "incorporate that culture into their own family's traditions" (13). Thus, while the adoptive family's shared life is enriched and expanded by honoring the culture from which their child came, it is still true that the child is drawn into "their own family's traditions." By virtue of the history of their relationship, those traditions have become the child's.

Similarly, there are ways in which Moore gives nuance to the position he has developed so straightforwardly. On the one hand, he asserts that the cultural heritage of his two adopted sons is no longer Russian but Mississippian. Yet, the very theological premises that ground his viewpoint require a certain qualification. For in the end, he clearly believes, the heritage of Christians is determined by their incorporation into Christ. "Whether our background is Norwegian or Haitian or Indonesian, if we are united to Christ, our family genealogy is found not primarily in the front pages of our dusty old family Bible but inside its pages, in the first chapter of the Gospel of Matthew. Our identity is in Christ; so his people are our people, his God our God" (37). Taken as seriously as Moore surely means this, however, it must mean that the fundamental heritage of his sons is neither Russian nor Mississippian in any simple sense. The story that tells who they are is the story the Bible tells. And perhaps when their lives are located within that story, there may be room for ways in which their identity is marked by both the Russia of their natural birth and the Mississippi of their history.

As we might expect, Moore and Sauer agree on a great deal. Nevertheless, their emphases do differ. For Sauer the bonds of nature are stronger than they are for Moore, whereas for Moore the meaning of a shared history trumps nature and biology more fully than Sauer thinks it does. Taken together, their contrasting positions pose for us a problem in need of continued reflection.

PUZZLE III

"Traditional Muslim law does not appear to allow formal adoption because it refuses to accept the legal fiction which an adoption creates, namely that an adopted child can become equal to a blood relative of the adopting father."[14] Indeed, so strong is the emphasis in Islam on the blood relation that no history of relationship, however long enduring, can efface it. When an adopted son reaches puberty, his adoptive mother will have to veil herself in his presence, and no physical intimacy, such as hugs or kisses, will be permitted between them. When an adopted daughter reaches puberty, she will need to veil herself in the presence of her adoptive father, and, here again, no physical intimacy will be permitted. Similar reasoning underlies Islamic objections to assisted reproduction techniques that use donor gametes or surrogacy, because they obscure a child's knowledge of his or her genetic "parents."

The significance of the blood tie can be seen in the story about Muhammad and a slave boy named Zayd, whom he adopted. Despite the adoption, after Zayd had divorced his wife, Muhammad married her. This was considered permissible precisely because there was no biological tie between Muhammad and Zayd. This action emphasized for Muslims "the difference between real parenthood and adoption, since marriage to a woman who has ever been married to one's son is forbidden" in the Qur'an.[15]

This does not mean that adoption is forbidden, or even frowned upon, in Muslim cultures. Indeed, it is commended as admirable, but what is commended is closer to what we would call foster care than to what we call adoption. To some extent the reasons for this are less theological than historical. In pre-Islamic Arab societies "adoption was closely linked to enslavement, which gave captors the power to strip captives of their natal identities and appropriate them into their own families."[16] It is not hard to understand why thinking of adoption in that context would place it under a cloud of suspicion. But something more like foster care, in which parents accept responsibility for and rear a child in need of a home, is approved and recommended by Muslims. Even so, this bond, however long extended, is neither a substitute nor a replacement for the biological bond between parents and child. The "adopted" child's identity remains distinct and is in no way absorbed into that of the adoptive family.

Thus, Islamic thought commends a relation that is something like permanent foster care while, at the same time, denying that any adoptive relation could efface the significance of the blood relation. Taken together, these two views can create tensions within Islamic thought. Compare, for example, two somewhat different definitions of adoption offered by Muslim sources. In the *Encyclopedia of Women & Islamic Cultures* adoption is defined as "the creation of a fictive relationship of parent to child, by naming the child as one's own and by endowing him or her with rights and duties identical to those of a biological child."[17] Somewhat different in tone—free of any language about "fictive" relationships—is the definition offered in a position paper of the Muslim Women's Shura Council: "the legal creation of a parent-child relationship, with all the responsibilities and privileges thereof, between a child and adults who are not his or her biological parents. Adoptions incorporate a child into a family as offspring and sibling, regardless of genetic ties."[18] Arguing for a more positive evaluation of adoption, the Shura Council suggests that the central concern of Islamic law is "dissimulation." That is, adoptions should be "open" in the sense that the child's familial origins (whenever known) should not be concealed even as the adoptive parents seek to integrate the child "to the fullest extent into the adoptive family."[19] Clearly, the relation between nature and history is complicated in Islamic thought about familial bonds.

It is likewise complicated in Judaism (at least for Orthodox Jews). Consider a thought experiment offered by Rabbi Michael Gold:

> Imagine two babies, one born to a Gentile woman and the other to a Jewish woman, and then exchanged at birth. The Gentile baby is raised in a Jewish home to be a committed, even observant, Jew. The Jewish baby is raised in a Christian home, knowing nothing of its biological origins. Later in life the truth comes out. By Jewish law, the way that the child is raised is irrelevant, the child born a Jew will be considered a Jew, the child born a Gentile remains a Gentile. In Judaism, biology is everything.[20]

To be sure, to read Rabbi Gold is to realize that he does not, in fact, think that biology is quite "everything" in Jewish thought. But it is a great deal. To be a Jew, one must either be born of a Jewish mother or undergo conversion. Moreover, one born of a Jewish mother simply is a Jew—whether he knows it or not, whether he accepts it or not. In our world, in which assisted reproduction procedures are gradually becoming more widespread, this can lead to puzzles for which there is no obvious solution. For example, suppose an infertile Jewish couple hires a gestational surrogate (who happens not to be Jewish) to bear a child produced in the laboratory by joining their sperm and ovum. The baby has a natural, genetic tie to the husband and wife, but no such tie to the woman who serves as the surrogate. Nevertheless, if the procedure succeeds, the child of these Jewish parents—a child born to a gentile woman—cannot easily be said to be Jewish unless the child undergoes conversion.[21]

Although, like Muslims, they emphasize the significance of the blood tie, Jews' central concern has less to do with what is permitted in sexual relationships than with defining who truly is a Jew. But the emphasis on biology does affect what is permitted or prohibited with respect to sexual bonds. So, for example, the laws governing *yichud* hold that a man and a woman who are not married should not be privately secluded with each other, since they could view each other as possible sexual partners. Parents are, however, permitted to be alone with their biological children; for, after all, the taboo against incest is strong enough to serve as protection here. What about seclusion with an adopted child of the opposite sex? It is hard to place within a Jewish framework, and halachic authorities have, it seems, disagreed about whether close physical contact with adopted children is permitted.[22]

But it is identity as a Jew, membership in the Jewish people, that most clearly raises the problem of nature and history. "Jewish law articulates the fundamental inability of a governing body to destroy essential parental relationships created at birth."[23] A gentile child who was adopted by Jewish parents and was to be raised as a Jew would need, as I noted, to undergo a conversion ceremony in order to be recognized as a Jew. That conversion, while it would make the child a Jew rather than a gentile, would not completely undo the effects of biological lineage. So, for example, an adopted child who has undergone conversion to Judaism is permitted to reject his conversion and relinquish his Jewish identity when he reaches the age for Bar Mitzvah, whereas this would be a kind of ontological impossibility for one who had been born a Jew. More thought-provoking still, Rabbi Gold, who is father to both an adopted son and an adopted daughter, notes that strictly speaking, "our son and daughter, although raised in the same household, would be permitted by Jewish law to marry one another since they are not consanguineous."[24] (I think, however, that this is more a theoretical than a real possibility, noted by Rabbi Gold not because of its likelihood but in order to demonstrate the fact that Jewish law does not have an institution of adoption as our society practices it.)

If it is not quite right to say that "biology is everything" in Judaism, it is true that the natural tie has profound and continuing effects. "For a people which intuitively perceives the importance of generations of connectedness, through blood and mutual history, it can," Shelley Kapnek Rosenberg writes, "be emotionally difficult to bestow full membership on one who does not share that connectedness."[25] One wonders, though, whether this can do justice to the feelings adoptive Jewish parents are likely to have toward their adopted children. As one such father writes: "The notion that I am doing a deed of kindness to a stranger is not what I feel; I feel him, unequivocally, to be my own son."[26] He experiences in his life the difficulties of relating nature and history.

Within Jewish tradition the influential thought of Rabbi Joseph Soloveitchik offers a way to recognize the significance of biological lineage while also placing it within a more expansive framework. He distinguishes two kinds of parenthood in his essay "Parenthood: Natural and Redeemed."[27] For Soloveitchik, a new kind of fatherhood appears with Abraham—a fatherhood that is responsive "not only to biological pressure but to the call of conscience" (107). The father becomes a teacher, charged with passing on the covenantal tradition to the next generation. Something similar happens to motherhood in the redeemed community. "Sarah became the first mother in the sense that her motherhood stemmed not only from instinctual involvement due to biological pressure but from free commitment as well" (108).

This widens the reach of fatherhood and motherhood, for, "elevated to a universal spiritual level," it is no longer "rooted in biological facticity" (108). From this perspective Rabbi Soloveitchik can even make a virtue of the fact that Judaism has had no practice of adoption. "The Romans—to whom the idea of covenant was alien, who, in spite of their advanced technological achievements, never freed themselves from the bonds of the natural community—tried to compensate the childless man and woman by establishing the institution of adoption. Judaism did not need to create such an institution" (109). Of course, this does not mean that nature makes no claims within the covenantal community. The natural tie of parents to child is "not liquidated or eliminated, since there is no power in the world which can nullify God's will" (111). Rather, it is redeemed, infused with new meaning and purpose. In that sense Abraham is the father of many peoples, with a fatherhood that "surpasses by far fatherhood due to a natural process of fertilization of the ovum" (121). The people who become children of Abraham and Sarah are, then, not simply a "clan" having a common biological ancestor; they are a redeemed, covenantal community (124).

This does not, of course, overturn the subtle distinctions between nature and history in Jewish law, but it gives them a greater theological depth and complexity. What it will not quite do, however, is address the competing claims of nature and history with respect specifically to adoption. For when motherhood and fatherhood are elevated by Rabbi Soloveitchik to a universal spiritual level, they refer less to specific children with whom one shares a familial history than to spiritual roles in the life of the redeemed community.

In a somewhat different way from Soloveitchik's, spiritual parenthood also receives emphasis in Christian thought. How this happens may be seen if we look very briefly at a talk given by Pope John Paul II at a meeting of adoptive families organized in September 2000 by the Missionaries of Charity, the order founded by Mother Teresa.[28] This talk was given on the occasion of the jubilee year of the order and on the third anniversary of the death of Mother Teresa.

At the outset John Paul reflects upon the fact that she was known as "Mother" Teresa, though, of course, she had never given birth. "A mother," the pope says, "is recognized by her ability to give herself." Hence, taking the anniversary as an occasion for remembering Mother Teresa's work of self-giving may help us all to "understand what it meant to her, beyond the purely physical dimension, to be a mother; it helped her get to the *spiritual root of motherhood*."

Against the background of the centrality of the natural, biological tie in Islamic and (with important qualifications) Jewish thought, this emphasis on motherhood as an essentially spiritual bond is striking. No doubt more needs to be said, and no doubt on some other occasion the pope might have provided that added nuance, but just as clearly he has placed something other than natural procreation alone at the heart of the relation between parents and children. In this context—an address delivered to a meeting of adoptive families—John Paul notes that one of the services nurtured by Mother Teresa's movement has been adoption, which he describes as a kind of great exchange in love. Adoptive parents (who may well be infertile) give much to the child whom they adopt, and in turn they find their desire to be mother or father to a child fulfilled.

"Adopting children, regarding and treating them as one's own children, means recognizing that the relationship between parents and children is not measured only by genetic standards." The pope is quite clear that, however highly and rightly we may exalt the natural, biological bond, the tie established through a shared familial history is every bit as profound, significant, and enduring. Indeed, he says precisely that: "The resulting relationship [i.e., after adoption] is so intimate and enduring that it is in no way inferior to one based on a biological connection."

More needs to be said. For example, when John Paul says, "There is a form of 'procreation' which occurs through acceptance, concern, and devotion," we might wonder whether, in order to underscore the moral significance of the love shown in adoption, it is necessary (or correct) to characterize it as procreation. In any case, puzzles remain, and it is clear that some of those puzzles may be theological in character. The claims of nature and history in forming the bond of children and parents are treated somewhat differently in these three religious traditions, presenting us with a problem for reflection.

PUZZLE IV

We need not turn to the world of high culture, to works of George Eliot, to be invited to think about complicated issues. Some of the most profound books are the short picture books written to be read to young children, and we should not be surprised to find our problem—the puzzling interaction of nature and history in parenthood—treated in such books.

In P. D. Eastman's *Are You My Mother?* the claims of nature are given their due.[29] The story begins with a mother bird sitting on an egg in her nest. The egg jumps, and the mother realizes that her baby will soon be there and will need to eat. She flies off in search of food. While she is gone, the baby bird hatches and finds himself alone. "Where is my mother?" he says. And that simple question generates a search that occupies the rest of the short book.

Off the baby bird goes, looking for his mother, even though he is not yet able to fly. Not quite knowing what his mother looks like, he can do no more than ask those he meets whether they by chance might be his mother. We meet possible but (for the reader) unlikely candidates in page after page—kitten, hen, dog, cow, car, boat, plane. None of them responds affirmatively, and so the search continues.

At last the baby bird sees a big steam shovel. Caught up in its huge shovel, he is lifted high into the air and dropped back into the nest in the tree from which his search had begun. "Just then the mother bird came back to the tree. 'Do you know who I am?' she said to her baby." And, of course, he does. He knows that she is not a kitten, hen, dog, or any of the other possible candidates he has met along the way. "You are a bird, and you are my mother." Although they have not yet really shared any time together, the baby bird has found the right mother for him, the mother naturally suited for him. And all is well, with mother and baby bird safely nestled together once again in their nest.

Are You My Mother? is an engaging story, but, at least for this reader, perhaps not as good a story to read to one's child as *A Mother for Choco*, written by Keiko Kasza.[30] In a sense, they are almost the same story, but in reverse. Choco is a little yellow bird with striped feet, who lives alone. "He wished he had a mother, but who could his mother be? One day he set off to find her."

We are treated to roughly the same sort of search. Choco meets a giraffe, but, lacking wings, she says she cannot be his mother. He meets a penguin, who does have wings but does not have big round cheeks like Choco's. He meets a walrus. She has the needed round cheeks but lacks the striped feet. Still other animals—an elephant, a turtle, a rabbit—are pictured. But "no matter where Choco searched, he couldn't find a mother who looked just like him."

Then Choco sees Mrs. Bear picking apples. He's sure she cannot be his mother, for she looks nothing at all like him. He starts to cry, and Mrs. Bear comes running to comfort him. "As she listened to Choco's story, she sighed. 'Oh, dear. If you had a mommy, what would she do?'"

She would hold me, Choco says. And Mrs. Bear hugs him tight.

She would kiss me, Choco says. "'Like this?' asked Mrs. Bear. And she lifted Choco and gave him a big kiss."

She would sing and dance with me, Choco says. And Mrs. Bear sings and dances with him.

Perhaps, Mrs. Bear suggests, she could be Choco's mother. But, says Choco, "You aren't yellow. And you don't have wings, or big, round cheeks, or striped feet like me!" True enough, acknowledges Mrs. Bear, but nonetheless she takes Choco home with her, where an apple pie and her other children are waiting. Those other children, who rush out to greet her, turn out to be a hippopotamus, an alligator, and a pig. They eat the pie and laugh and sing together.

"After their delicious treat, Mrs. Bear gave all her children a big, warm bear hug. And Choco was very happy that his new mommy looked just the way she did."

Here the claims of a shared history are given their due, and, differences of nature notwithstanding, who would not want a mother like Mrs. Bear? The two children's stories, similar in so many ways, tilt in different directions when weighing the claims of nature and history. And we are left to puzzle over which we would choose to read to our children.

Four puzzling examples, each in its own way inviting us to see in adoption an instance within the moral life of the relation between nature and history. To return to where I began: it does not seem quite right to refuse to recognize that Laius and Jocasta are parents to Oedipus. Nor does it seem quite right to call them his parents. Nature and history meet uneasily in adoption. And, as an exchange in love, adoption makes clear that the claims of nature must be markedly qualified, even if they should never be denied.

Thinking through his own experience as an adoptive father, Russ Richter offers a perceptive observation about two different meanings of the word *cleave*.[31] In some contexts it means "to split apart" or "to separate." In other contexts it means "to hold close together." The first might be taken as a description of a biological child's entry into his or her family, separating from the mother's body. The second might remind us of how an adopted child enters into the adoptive family, being drawn into close relation with his or her parents. Richter then notes the crucial point:

"The resultant bond created by this *cleaving of children* is indistinguishable between the two 'cleaving' methods."[32] Therefore, as John Berkman has suggested, we should learn to think of parenting as a "covenantal" task. The important question is not whether parents are biological or adoptive. The important question is whether they understand themselves to have covenanted with their children in a way that determines the future course of their life together. Thus, as Berkman puts it, true parents, whether biological or adoptive, are those who "have lived out the long-term commitment to parent."[33]

Interlude I
Gifts and Achievements

Dear Derek:

I have not forgotten the day we learned that you would be coming to live with us. I was sitting in my office at Oberlin and Mom called. She said that Children Services had a three-month-old boy who was due to come out of the hospital but could not be sent home to his biological parents. They needed to place him in a foster home and wanted to know if we'd take him.

At the time, we were only doing foster care for preadoptive infants, and you were not one. Still, though you didn't fit the profile, there you were. Ready to leave the hospital, needing a home. And the question was: would we take you? Mom and I talked it over, and I can still remember saying to her, just as casually as I might comment on the weather, "Well, if you want to, it's OK with me."

Here we are, eighteen years later, and it's still OK with me. But I have often thought about that moment, about how casually I made what turned out to be a lifelong commitment, and about how such moments shape our lives. I'll want to say more about that. For today, though, I want to write words about both the debt of thanks you owe to others and the pride you should take in where you've come.

You were, you know, born very prematurely, and you had a rough start in life that left you behind in lots of ways. For a long time I wasn't sure you could ever catch up. Clearly, you have, but you didn't accomplish it on your own. I'm not sure any little child ever got more attention from older brothers and sisters than you got from Peter, Ellen, and Hannah. Peter throwing the ball to you time after time and then chasing it down when you threw it who-knows-where. Ellen and Hannah playing games with you for hours on end. But for all the thanks you owe them, you owe still more to Mom. It would be impossible to count the hours she devoted to you—driving you to therapists, reading up on your problems, giving you attention in the countless ways that you needed to catch up and, then, to flourish.

In short, you owe a considerable debt of gratitude to others for where you've come today. You couldn't have done it without them, but it's also true that you've done it. We're proud of the person you've become—and you should be too. You have accomplished a great deal through sheer force of will and perseverance. You can picture it a little like those moving belts in the airport. Because the belt moves as you walk along it, your rate of progress depends on its help. But still, if you want to move along quickly, you yourself have to walk.

I hope over the years you'll keep both of these truths in mind: that you owe much to others, and that we give you credit for what you've achieved. And really, you know, even though your case is special because you were adopted, both of these lessons are true for all of us. We're all indebted from the start, before we are even able to form the words "thank you." There's really no repaying such debts. All we can do is be grateful.

One way we show that gratitude is precisely by applying ourselves—as you have done. We don't waste all the help we've received. We're most likely not to do that when we learn to recognize even our greatest achievements as, finally, gifts from others and from God. It's not that there are some things you received from others for which you must be thankful—and other things that you've accomplished on your own. No. The very things you accomplish are also the gifts of others. And the point of those gifts is precisely that you should live and flourish. I trust that you will.

Love,

Dad

(*Christian Century*, June 28, 2003)

CHAPTER 2

Adoptees One and All

Discussing the command in the Decalogue that children should honor their parents, Karl Barth writes: "It is not with this physical relationship as such that the command is concerned, but with a certain oversight and responsibility with regard to the children which this physical relationship implies for the parents. This oversight and responsibility does not belong to the physical but, broadly speaking, to the historical order."[1] In asserting this Barth by no means intends to downplay the significance of the natural relationship between biological parent and child. He does, after all, also say that fatherhood and motherhood "confer a *character indelebilis.*"[2] Even acknowledging that, however, Christians should affirm that the bond between parent and child must be formed over time by their shared history.

ADOPTION AS SONS

Although it does not occur frequently, the language of adoption is of great significance in the New Testament. The

Greek word *huiothesia*, sometimes translated "adoption," or "adoption as a son," but more literally as "placing [someone] as a son," occurs relatively few times in the Pauline letters, but it characterizes the way in which one comes to live "in Christ" and, through him, as a child of his Father.[3] So, for example, in Ephesians 1:5 believers are told that through Jesus they have been destined in love for *huiothesia*, for adoption as sons. Similarly, in Romans 8:23 St. Paul writes that, living in a world that is in bondage to decay and suffering the pangs of childbirth, we live in hope as we wait for the promised "adoption as sons."

Because Jewish tradition had no legal practice of adoption, it is likely that Paul's use of the language of adoption had Roman law as its background. And, as Trevor Burke notes, the Pauline letters use the metaphor of *huiothesia* "only in letters to communities directly under the rule of Roman law."[4] The purpose of adoption in Roman law was not to benefit the child adopted but to ensure that the family line would continue.[5] Yet, of course, there were also important consequences for the person adopted. In Roman law, Francis Lyall writes, "the adoptee is taken out of his previous state and is placed in a new relationship with his new paterfamilias. All his old debts are canceled, and in effect he starts a new life."[6]

Such a practice seems to lie in the background when Paul writes in Romans 8:14–15 that believers, having received the Spirit of God, received not a spirit of slavery but the Spirit of adoption, making them, like Christ, sons who can cry, "Abba! Father!" A similar pattern of thought appears in chapter 4 of Galatians. God sent his Son, Paul writes, for the sake of those who were enslaved by "the elemental spirits of the universe"— in order that they might be redeemed, receive *huiothesia*, and, living by the Spirit of Christ, cry out, "Abba! Father!"

It is no legal fiction that Paul has in mind.[7] What the Spirit's work of *huiothesia* does is give the place—the genuine place— of a son to one to whom that place does not belong by nature. That is, the adoptee's sonship is not assured "by natural descent or merit," but is "a sonship always dependent on God's free grace."[8] Even God's chosen people, Israel, is so not by nature but by covenant. Their status also, Paul writes in Romans 9:4, is one of *huiothesia*, as John the Baptist made clear when he taught that it was not sufficient for Israelites to appeal to Abraham as their Father.[9] Therefore, it is not as if gentile Christians are incorporated into God's people on a basis different from that of Jewish believers; all receive the Spirit-given adoption as sons.[10] Of all people it is true, as St. Paul writes in 1 Corinthians 15:50, that flesh and blood will not inherit the kingdom.

In this way Paul relativizes biological fatherhood without denying its significance. God's fatherhood comes first; ours is a reflection and imitation. Thus, in Ephesians 3:14–15 the apostle says that all other fatherhood, whether in heaven or on earth, takes its name from the Father before whom we should bend the knee.[11] In our created nature we can already be called children of the God who has made us and all that is; thus, in the famous speech of Paul on the Areopagus, as it is recounted in Acts, we are said to be "God's offspring."[12] But that creation only points toward a deeper relation, characterized by the Pauline letters as "sonship." In Jesus God does more than just restore the integrity of the creation that has been corrupted by sin. He reveals, as Karl Barth put it, "a perfection concealed even in the original creation in its integrity."[13] What is concealed comes to fulfillment in the *huiothesia* worked by the Spirit of Christ, enabling us now to name the Creator as our Father. This identity is given not in nature but in history, in the history of God's work of redemption. No one can claim it simply by virtue of his or her created nature.

In this connection we should recall the significance for Christians of baptism as a means by which one becomes a child of God. That significance is especially powerful when parents bring a newborn child for baptism, handing over—indeed, relinquishing—that child. Deeply bound as they are to this child by ties of biology, gestation, and birth, the child is not theirs to possess. Indeed, Michael Banner has recently noted the moral implications of the role of godparents as that office developed centuries ago, although it has now lost much of its traditional meaning.[14] The origins of the practice are not entirely clear, and it varied some-what from place to place and time to time, but by the early Middle Ages it was often the case that the child was presented for baptism by the godparents. In some places the parents were expected to be absent from the baptism, and relatives were sometimes forbidden to be godparents.

Why? Because an "intensification of 'natural' kinship which occurs with the use of relatives in this role was fundamentally at odds with a practice which sought not to intensify existing kinship, but to displace or relativize it."[15] This did not mean that natural kinship was of no significance, but it did mean that Christians had to rework their understanding of it. Baptism is not primarily an event of importance for the biological family, even if relatives of the child are generally present. Rather, it signifies that at the deepest level the child's identity is marked by relation to God, who sets his hand upon us in baptism and calls us by name. The baptized person is destined for a greater family than the one into which he was born—a destiny that comes not through natural bonds but through *huiothesia*. Hence, all Christian parents must relinquish their children for adoption, and we are (one and all) adoptees.[16]

A Theological Framework

To know ourselves as God's adopted children we must see ourselves within the history of God's redeeming work. That history does not ignore the significance of our created nature, but it also sees us as people on the way toward the greater destiny of God's new creation. This requires that we understand human life not as static but as always "on the way"—and, hence, characterized by the several forms of God's activity that shape this history.

A useful framework for thinking of this history of redemption is the one provided by Karl Barth in the massive (and never completed) volumes of his *Church Dogmatics*. He offers there an account of human life that corresponds to the threefold form of God's action in creation, reconciliation, and redemption.[17] Because we are God's creatures, we must acknowledge, honor, and even celebrate the human nature that is ours. Because we are (pardoned) sinners whom God has in Jesus acted to reconcile, we must come to terms with the countless ways in which human life is disordered and broken. And because we are heirs of the future God has promised, we must live toward a destiny that will fulfill and transform our created nature without simply obliterating it. If we take this threefold structure seriously, we will not deny the significance of biological ties, we will not deny the pain and sorrow that is often embedded in the circumstances that lead to adoption, and we will not deny that our identity as God's children is in the end determined not by biology alone but also by adoption. In short, we cannot say just one thing or think within just one perspective and expect thereby to do justice to a person's identity.

Complex though Barth's approach may be, it is a complexity that corresponds to the nature of human life before God, and it is to be preferred to an approach that would isolate any single point in this history of redemption and allow it to define our identity without remainder. It is worth noting several ways in which we might make that mistake.

Ted Peters's rejection of what he calls an "inheritance myth" is an example of one way to lose the needed complexity. This myth, as he describes it, "seeks ethical grounding in our biological inheritance—rather than in the new eschatological future that God has promised."[18] Noting that in the Old Testament God becomes Israel's father not by procreation but by covenantal adoption, and that Jesus seems to expand our understanding of family bonds well beyond the genetic (as in Matthew 12:46–50), Peters argues that the moral meaning of our relationships is determined by where God is taking us, not where we have come from. "Spirit transcends biology. We pass from being people of dust to people of heaven." And, hence, our identity is determined by "the network of relations that will constitute the Kingdom of God."[19] Even today, therefore, we need not think of our identity as marked in any significant way by our biological origins. We may create familial bonds in countless different ways, all equally good if our vision is shaped by God's eschatological future. Peters's aim, in short, is that our decisions about how to produce children should be in no way limited by our created nature. As Don Browning puts it, for Peters "the transformations of God's kingdom that come from the future are totally disconnected from creation and nature."[20] That cannot be an adequate Christian account.

Moved by a very different brand of Christian piety, one might make a mistake not unlike the one Peters makes by seeming (at least at times) to suppose that biological origins have no significance for personal identity. Thus, for example, Russ Richter writes of his adoptive children: "My daughters understand that, even though they grew in another mommy's tummy, that [sic] they were made specifically and exclusively for our family. We have equated their abandonment with a letter being placed in a mailbox. In other words, they were not discarded by their birth mothers. Instead, they were sent on a journey to us, their forever family."[21] Those who think this way have also sometimes thought of adoption as carrying out the church's mission to bring the gospel to those who have not heard it. This cannot be quite right, however, for both the metaphor of *huiothesia* and the significance of baptism make clear that simply bringing a child into a Christian home does not in itself guarantee that he will come to faith. That is God's work and beyond our power to manipulate.[22]

There are other ways to lose the needed complexity. Rather than making the promised future the focal point of our identity, we might suppose that the parent-child bond requires a basis in genetic and biological ties. So, for example, Melissa Moschella argues that children have an interest in being loved by their biological parents and that "strictly speaking, no one else can replace biological parents in this regard."[23] Moschella articulates this position chiefly in order to argue against third-party gamete donation in assisted reproduction, but in so doing she comes close to undermining the true character of adoption. In my view, her argument takes a wrong turn at the outset by regarding a gamete donor as a parent who has procreated. If there is something morally problematic about gamete donation, as I think there is, it does not depend on seeing the donor as a parent or characterizing donation as procreation. I'm unsure what it means, then, when Moschella writes (with gamete donors in mind), "Even if they have never actually met, biological parents are *not* strangers to their children." Strangers, even if genetic kin, would seem to be precisely what they are.

For to be father or mother to a child requires an orientation to the future, to a shared history and a life together. Perhaps this is often more evident to mothers than fathers, for mothers have from the start shared not just a genetic connection but nine months of gestational intimacy. For fathers it may require what Gabriel Marcel called "an engagement and a decision," making fatherhood something that goes well beyond procreation alone.[24] Understanding the importance of this orientation toward a future shared history enables us "to understand the metaphysical foundation of adoption, and to recognise that it is not merely a pale and bloodless copy of real fatherhood, but that it can be a means of grace, destined to make up for the deficiencies of biological filiation."[25] For St. Augustine, the paradigmatic example of one whose engagement and decision made him a father was Joseph, who, Augustine tells his listeners in a sermon, was a father to Jesus "not by the flesh but by love. So he is indeed a father, in his own proper way."[26]

Yet a third way in which we might lose some of the complexity present in Barth's three angles of vision could happen if, in order to underscore the ways in which adoption can be a blessing for all involved, we fail to do justice to the brokenness and disorder of life. Even when the good of all parties is served—when a birth mother, knowing herself unable to care for her child, gives the child up for adoption; when adoptive parents understand themselves not just as satisfying their own desires but as coming to the aid of the birth mother; and when the child thereby receives a family as a place of belonging and nurture—there will still be loss and costs to be borne.

When we remember the stories of "barren wombs" in the Old Testament, women who for a time mourned their inability to conceive—Sarah, Rachel, Hannah—we will see that the claims of our created nature are powerfully connected with our sense of who we are. Or when a birth mother in love gives up her child for adoption, we do still speak of her "relinquishing" the child, testifying to a brokenness not entirely effaced. Jeremy Cook, reflecting upon the experience he and his wife have as parents of adopted twins from Kenya, acknowledges that brokenness, when he writes: "I wonder if in some strange way we honor their birth mother by acknowledging the pain. As deep as the joy is from our adoption, this is not some fairy tale. She lost profoundly, and we have gained immensely."[27] Likewise, thinking from the perspective of the child adopted, William Werpehowski has urged that, even when a child is relinquished to a family that becomes a place of love and belonging, the child too must incur some "moral cost."[28]

Werpehowski's point is made in a rejoinder to Stephen Post's expressed concerns about a kind of "genealogical essentialism" that tends to depreciate the value of adoption and to encourage adoptees to search for their genetic roots.[29] Post is not claiming that there are simply two equally choiceworthy ways for parents to see to the rearing of children born to them—namely, by rearing the children themselves or by giving them up for adoption. He does, however, intend to affirm that there are "limited ranges of circumstances" when normal parental duties are rightly relinquished in favor of adoption. And when that is the case, the adoptive parent-child relation is, he suggests, in no way inferior.[30] Werpehowski's response is intended less as disagreement than as nuance. He suggests that if we honor the created bond between parents and children, we will set it aside only when there is special reason for doing so—and, hence, there will always be some moral cost experienced by all the parties involved. From a similar perspective Elizabeth Kirk writes that a mother who gives up her child for adoption "does not abandon her child. Rather, she first gives her child life, in an age in which to choose this is a heroic virtue."[31] Hence, the way to respond to our world's brokenness is not to turn against adoption but to acknowledge that before God all parents are adoptive parents, who should receive their children as gifts and blessings, recognizing that "the lives of their children are not their own."[32] If we teach ourselves to think in that way, we will know, as Kirk puts it, that those who adopt do so "always in service to" the birth parents and "for the child."[33]

In short, if we isolate any single moment in the history of redemption, taking it as definitive of what it means to be parent or child, we are likely to go wrong. Of course, it is always easier to depict ways in which we might go wrong than it is to point out the right path. There is no single way to characterize that path; for, recognizing the wrong turns we might take does not mean that there is some single correct depiction of the bond between parents and children. What we can say, however, is that our vision must from the start be shaped by the deepest truth: namely, that we are, by grace and not by nature, adopted children of God. Knowing that, we will also know, as Michael Banner writes, that children "are only properly received when they are received as gifts from the hands of God—which is why adoption might have some claim to model an archetype of parenthood for those who are themselves children by adoption."[34]

If *huiothesia* is our starting point, it will not be sufficient to think of the family as just a genetic or biological bond. For if that were the sum and substance of the relation between parents and children, then, as Brent Waters has put it, adoption would be "inexplicable."[35] Nor can it be satisfactory to think of the family simply as a reproductive project—the result of our will and choice. For then adoption becomes, as Waters notes, "irrelevant"—just one reproductive option among many, but not the fundamental starting point for our vision.[36]

What is the better alternative? Whether the connection of child to parents is biological or adoptive, in each case God provides for the child a place of belonging—a place that looks back to the created good of the family, a place that offers an intimation of the redeemed community promised by God. Waters's characterization of the family as a place of belonging makes clear that a shared history is essential. "A boy, for example, may say that the woman who surrendered him for adoption is his mother and he is her son, but she is not the mother of the family in which he belongs."[37] To be sure, the adoptive family does not reject the created order but affirms its structure and helps to heal its brokenness. "An adoptive family is not a small orphanage."[38] Its form is patterned after that of the natural family, for it looks back to the creation.

Nevertheless, we should not think of adoption simply as an alternative way to satisfy one's desire to be a parent. It is intended not so much to satisfy our desires as to provide a child's needed place of belonging. Hence, rather than replacing the natural family, it restores the family's orientation toward the eschatological place of belonging that God has promised, making both biological and adoptive parenthood works of love, turning us in the direction of the redeemed community that is God's intention for the creation.

Failing to say something like this would mean that we were trying to understand the family without incorporating it into the history of redemption. And then, redemption would no longer be about our bodily and historical relationships—about the healing of their brokenness, about the fulfillment and completion of the goods they serve. We need to think of the relation between parents and children as one that is intended, in God's providence, to move toward a meaningful and fulfilling end. Beginning with *huiothesia* is the key to doing so.

EVERYDAY EXAMPLES

That Christians begin by thinking in New Testament terms of *huiothesia* does not mean they cannot learn from other ways of thinking. I offer here two examples in which people, reflecting on our experience of parent-child bonds, come to think in ways that support and reinforce a theological framework that makes "adoption as sons" central.

Emily Yoffe, writing as the advice columnist for the online publication *Slate*, offers her counsel in response to all sorts of questions. One such inquiry was the following from a high school student:

Dear Prudence,
My high school requires a senior project to graduate, and I chose to do one on genealogy. In my research I discovered that the woman who I always thought was my grandmother was in fact my stepgrandmother. She married my granddad when my mom was 6 years old and raised my mom as her own. The project required I trace all four of my biological grandparents. When I spoke to my grandfather about this, he requested that I drop that project and do something else. I did, but I love research and kept digging. I was able to find that my biological grandmother is on the list of names of the dead from a mass suicide cult. It turns out I have aunts, uncles, and a great-grandmother. My grandfather begged me to let it go and never tell my mom. He had told her years ago that her mother left because of a drinking and drug problem. I asked my mother if she ever thinks about her real mom and she smiled and said, "My real mom raised me, she loves me, you, and your brother. The woman who left a 5-year-old is not a real mom, and I don't think about her at all." Should I tell her there is living family while she still has time to meet them? The mystery of these other relatives is killing me.
—The Curious Cat[39]

In a technical sense, this query may not involve an instance of adoption, but it does not differ in ways that are significant for the issues I am considering.

How should a wise counselor reply in order to take account of the several different kinds of claims that the theological framework sketched above includes? At least by my lights Prudence does quite well with her reply. "Curious Cat" had asked whether she should tell her mother about the existence of biological relatives, and Prudence answers: "You in essence asked your mother the question and she gave you an eloquent answer about love and biology. She told you she knows who her real mother is and doesn't want to know more about her biological mother. You need to respect that." Perhaps that alone would have been sufficient answer, but, taken alone, it might not have adequately acknowledged Werpehowski's concept of "moral cost." And Prudence does say more. "You will soon be a young adult off at college. With your research skills, you could continue your investigation and from a distance find out quite a bit about the relatives you've never met. Before you decide on making contact, however, keep in mind the emotional consequences for others of forcing them to relive wrenching events that for you are simply a source of fascination." This is not, of course, theological reflection, but it is good advice not at all incompatible with the theological framework outlined above.

A second example, testifying clearly to the brokenness of our lives, is even more powerful. In February 2015 a story of two babies, born in France some twenty years ago and accidentally switched at birth, came to public attention.[40] One of the baby girls developed jaundice and was placed in an incubator. Because the hospital did not have enough cradles, she was placed in the same cradle as another naked baby—and, in the end, each newborn was given to the mother of the other. The parents of both children experienced some puzzlement, since even as infants the daughters given to them in the hospital bore very little physical resemblance to them.

It was a decade later before, because of a paternity test taken by the parents of one child, the mistake was uncovered and gradually unraveled. The two families made contact and saw each other a number of times. But, as the *New York Times* article reported, "the parents and daughters had trouble building any rapport. . . . In the end, after some discussion, both families preferred to keep the child they had raised, rather than taking their biological one." Sophie Serrano, mother of one of the children, said of the daughter to whom she was biologically related, "I realized that we were very different, and we didn't approach life in the same way. My biological daughter looked like me, but I suddenly realized that I had given birth to a person I didn't know and I was no longer the mother of that child."

It is only one story, of course, and one could take from it many different lessons. In such a story there is undeniable loss, and it is clear from the news report that all those involved—parents and children—have experienced that loss. But it is also clear that shared history—not just biology—can create a bond between parent and child. Thus, Ms. Serrano says, "What makes a family is what we build together, what we tell each other." We cannot simply wipe out our created nature and the bonds it involves. We cannot deny that the loss of those connections may be painful. But we should also not forget that the mutual love shared by father, mother, and child can shape a common history that begins to redeem the brokenness of human life, and points toward the future kingdom God promises.

FLESH AND BLOOD WILL NOT INHERIT THE KINGDOM

In the end, however, we need more than such everyday examples, helpful though they are. In his Preface to *Christian Ethics and the Church* Philip Turner recalls how a seminary professor of his had once said to him: "Where you come from [in my case Virginia], being an Episcopalian is something that happens in certain families."[41] But the thrust of the preface—and, indeed, of the entire book—is that the life of the church has its ground, as the Letter to the Ephesians depicts it, in the gracious purpose of God to restore in Christ the broken unity of the creation. And the fulfillment of that purpose is closely linked to the church's life. "The grace bestowed in Christ engenders love, and love in turn elicits praise."[42]

Turner recounts a story of what it means to live in an ecclesial community that genuinely understands itself as united not by flesh and blood but by adoption in Christ as God's children. At a "fellowship meeting" of a Ugandan church a young couple asked their fellow members for counsel. A new and better job possibility had opened up, which would entail a move from the countryside to the city. They had been told that living in the city would require them to take out an insurance policy on their property as protection against theft and that they would need a watchdog ferocious enough to defend them against attackers. They, however, worried that insurance was a way of refusing to heed Jesus's command to take no thought for the morrow and that procuring a watchdog would be a way of avoiding Jesus's command to turn the other cheek to one's enemies.

After discussion and prayer the elders of the fellowship offered their counsel: Even if they moved to the city, the couple should not get a watchdog, for that would be a failure to witness to Christ's love for both us *and* our enemies. But the insurance policy was judged permissible because, if they were robbed, they could no longer rely on the common life of their fellowship to care for them. "The congregation accepted this judgment, sang a hymn, and went home."[43] What was Turner's view? Though he disagreed (then and still today) on the matter of the watchdog, he was "stunned"—stunned "because it seemed then and still seems a judgment of remarkable depth."[44] Doubting that the churches in which he had grown up could be capable of such a judgment, he concluded that "Christian identity is the question for this time."[45]

At the heart of Christian identity is *huiothesia*. It can and should shape our understanding of the history of redemption and the meaning of our shared life within the church. For that fellowship is not founded on flesh and blood nor shaped definitively by the culture in which we find ourselves; in that community formed by God's grace we are, one and all, adoptees.

Interlude II

Living into Commitments

Dear Derek:

In my last letter I commented on how casually I said yes when Mom asked whether we should agree to have you come into our home as a foster child. A simple decision on a busy day, and it has shaped the rest of my life—and yours. This is worth our thinking about together.

Suppose I'd never said yes. How would my life be different? I'd have had more time to get my work done. I wouldn't, at this point in life, have responsibilities to a child who was still in school. (I still remember walking down the street with Mom for "back to school night" when you were in kindergarten. I just began laughing, hardly able to believe that I was starting all over again—admiring the art work, looking at the projects, and so forth.) I suppose if I'd not said yes I might have had a little more money to spend along the way, and Mom would certainly have had far more free time. (We also wouldn't have had a string of twenty-four consecutive years of children's piano recitals, which may be a few more than any human being needs. We would have been able to cut it off at a decent 18 years or so.)

But, of course, that's not all. I'd never have heard your cheerful "good morning"—so regularly and amazingly cheerful even at 6:00 a.m. (And, in general, I think I'd have suffered for not having such a cheerful person around me all these years.) I'd have missed years of playing "pepper" in the backyard with you (until my right elbow finally gave out). I'd never have seen a bedroom decorated for Halloween the way yours is. I'd never have realized that there are people who really see how things look, who can tell you where the chimney was on a house they saw once and can sketch the way the front of a building looked. It's not likely that I'd know who Kenny G is, nor that I'd have had anyone around who shared my simple joy of watching old videos and calling out (in advance) different lines.

In short, you've worked me hard (and are still working me hard), but I can't imagine that I'd have laughed nearly as much if you hadn't been around all these years.

There's a much more important point, though, for us to think about here. Much too often we suppose that the way to live is to think through what we want to do and then figure out how to do it. People talk constantly about setting goals. (Colleges and universities love to do this, except they get even more pretentious, talking about their "mission." How I dislike it.) Thinking this way does not really prepare us well for living as responsible people, because the truth is that life seldom works like that.

Much of the time we're already committed in important ways before we really decide what our goals should be. And, because we're already committed, other people have expectations based on those commitments. The trick of life is not to figure out who I am and then decide what sorts of commitments such a person should make. The trick is to become the person who can carry out the commitments I've already made. Don't imagine that the point of life is to set goals. Think, instead, that its point is to be faithful to the commitments already built into your life. People who make goals central are people who think the most important things in life are consciously chosen. People who make faithfulness central are people who realize that, quite often, our obligations come to us in ways that are unexpected, unchosen, and even unwanted.

You came into our home—and then you just stayed and stayed—a little, bald-headed kid with glasses. I didn't choose that or decide that things should be like that. But somewhere along the way I gradually realized that you'd become my son—and that, therefore, we had responsibilities to each other. The task—and the gift—then, is to recognize the fact and learn to live up to its inner meaning. I think we've managed that, and, speaking for myself, I hope I last long enough to work you as hard as you've worked me.

Love,
Dad
(*Christian Century*, July 12, 2003)

CHAPTER 3

Q & A

If we allow ourselves to puzzle over the different ways in which nature and history work to form families, and if we recognize that the centrality of adoption in the New Testament must shape our understanding of what it means to be a father or mother, a son or daughter, we will have come to see adoption as, at its heart, a theological matter. Even so, some other questions, common in discussions of adoption, are bound to occur to us. Leaving two of them, which seem to require more extended discussion, for the next two chapters, I here take up in briefer fashion a few of them.

Is adoption only for the infertile? A second-best substitute for couples who cannot have children?
In the prologue to *Adoption Nation*, a thorough and serious treatment of many important issues raised by the practice of adoption, Adam Pertman includes a cartoon by Don Wasserman, an editorial cartoonist. Picture a meeting, people standing around chatting, coffee cups in their hands. One of the women is obviously pregnant, and another says to her: "Oh, I'm sorry . . . You couldn't

adopt?" This is, Pertman comments, "an exaggerated view of reality, to be sure, but it reflects a fundamental truth"—namely, that adoption need not be a second and inferior choice.[1]

Should we endorse Pertman's comment? Certainly it is hard not to smile at Wasserman's witty cartoon, inverting as it does our common notion that adoption is a kind of second-best option for couples who cannot have children. And there is truth in the cartoon insofar as it invites us to consider that the relation between adoptive parents and their children may be in no way inferior to the bond that unites parents with their biological children.

Nevertheless, there is still something a little off the mark about Pertman's response. For the cartoon also seems to suggest that nothing would be amiss if married couples routinely bypassed procreation in favor of adoption, choosing it as their preferred route to parenthood. In such a world we would have lost something of importance in the goodness of God's creation—namely, the way in which God so often blesses the mutual self-giving of a husband and wife with the gift of a child. That child is God's "yes" to his creation, a sign that we give and receive love not simply for our own fulfillment but as part of God's continuing care for the world. Russell Moore effectively holds together the created priority of procreation with adoption patterned in its image when he writes: "You are indeed designed to love 'your own flesh and blood,' but your design is redeemed in Christ to see as your flesh and blood those whom you previously didn't recognize as such."[2]

Elizabeth Bartholet, who, like Pertman, is well known for her writing on adoption, also seems by my lights to go a step too far in her advocacy of adoption. Specifically addressing the question whether adoption should be thought of chiefly as an alternative approach to parenthood for those who are infertile, she says: "Adoption should not be seen simply as a partial solution for some of the world's social ills. Adoption should be understood as a positive alternative to the blood-based family form."[3] Bartholet is not wrong to suggest that the human need to nurture the next generation is at least as important as the need to procreate, but to think of adoption as more desirable than pro-creation is to begin to lose the moral significance of our bodily attachments.

We would not know the meaning of the parent-child bond were it not given to us in nature. Adoption, therefore, does not replace the natural family; rather, it is shaped and informed by it. Were that not the case—when that is not the case—we too easily come to think of the child as chosen by his or her parents. That, in fact, is one of the reasons Bartholet likes (and in some ways prefers) adoption. She prefers a world in which one does not become a parent by accident, in which being the child of certain parents is the result of having been consciously chosen. But how much this misses. A centrally important aspect of the moral life, and certainly of the meaning of parenthood, is learning to deal with the unwanted and unexpected in life.

In natural procreation the child is not consciously chosen—and is certainly not a product meeting certain specifications. On the contrary, husband and wife give themselves to each other in love, and sometimes that mutual exchange is blessed with the gift of a child. Even if they hoped that their lovemaking would be fruitful, the focus of their attention in the act was not choosing a child but giving and receiving love. They have not in the first place been engaged in a reproductive project, and that is precisely why the child can be received as a gift. If, on occasion, the child seems more like a burden than a blessing, an unchosen and oner-ous burden, they are given the opportunity to come to see this unwanted and unexpected task as their calling. And, of course, others of us are given the opportunity to help them rise to meet the challenges of that calling.

None of this is to deny that a fertile couple might for good reasons decide to become parents by means of adoption, seeing this as the vocation to which they have been called, and for that reason setting their natural procreative powers to the side. Seeing children who need not just a place to live but a family to which they belong, seeing children with special needs and believing themselves suited to meet those needs, they might rightly turn to adoption as the way to become parents together. But there is a world of difference between such a sense of calling and supposing that adoption is a desirable alternative to procreation because it more clearly involves conscious choice to become a parent of a particular child. Thus, Marcel is right to say *both* that adoption "can be a means of grace, destined to make up for the deficiencies of biological filiation," *and* that in any healthy society it "must always be exceptional."[4]

Whose good is chiefly served by adoption—that of the adoptive parents, the adopted child, or the birth parents?

In an address to a meeting of adoptive families, Pope John Paul II once said: "To adopt a child is a great *work of love*. When it is done, much is given, but much is also received. It is a true exchange of gifts."[5] That is, in my view, a wonderfully perceptive statement, enunciating a truth that lies at the heart of adoption. But compare it to words spoken by Philippa Palfrey, the central character in P. D. James's novel *Innocent Blood*. Philippa, an adopted child who wants to learn the identity of her biological parents, is speaking with the case worker who must approve her request.

> "If I needed to adopt, and I never would, the last thing I'd want would be a child selected for me by a social worker. If we didn't take to each other I wouldn't be able to hand it back without the social services department striking me off the books as being one of those neurotic self-indulgent women who want a child for their own satisfaction. And what other possible reason could there be for wanting an adopted child?"
>
> "Perhaps to give that child a better chance."
>
> "Don't you mean, to have the personal satisfaction of giving that child a better chance? It amounts to the same thing."[6]

For John Paul the marvel of adoption is that the interests of the adoptive parents and the interests of the adopted child may coincide. The interests of both parties are served; yet, the exchange is not a self-interested one. For Philippa Palfrey there is no such mutuality. We may talk as if we have the child's best interests at heart, but the good being served is really that of adoptive parents who desire a child.

Moreover, as someone will quickly point out, whether we are more inclined to the view of John Paul or that of Philippa, an important third party has been left out of consideration—namely, the birth parents (most often, though not always, the birth mother). There have, of course, been instances in both domestic and international adoption in which a birth mother's agreement to relinquish her child for adoption has not really been freely given (because of deception or, even, coercion). But even when that is not the case, the interests of birth parents must also be considered.

From one angle we might say that all parties involved have experienced or will experience loss. If, as will most often be the case, the adoptive parents are infertile, they may well grieve at their inability to procreate. We would be missing something if we simply said to them, "Oh well, you can always adopt." Birth parents, and perhaps most especially birth mothers, may feel that their stage in life or their financial circumstances make it impossible to raise their child—and may suffer from the loss of that bond, even if they believe it is best for their child to be adopted. The child adopted will have lost the tie with his or her biological parents, a connection established in the creation. That this loss can be transformed through the grace of adoption does not mean that no loss is involved.

At the same time, we should recognize that there is gain as well as loss for all three parties involved. First and foremost, children in need of loving parental nurture are given a chance to receive it. The good of all parties may be served, but adoption exists first for the sake of the well-being of children. Birth parents can grieve the loss of their child while knowing that they have helped that child to find a place of belonging. They do not cease, in one important sense, to be parents of that child, but they can take some reassurance from knowing that adoptive parents have come to their aid, standing in for them in a place they cannot fill. We should teach ourselves to see that, in Elizabeth Kirk's words, "the mother who chooses adoption does not abandon her child. Rather, she first gives her child life."[7] And, even while satisfying the deep human impulse to nurture the next generation, adoptive parents may be taught a truth all parents need to learn—namely, that our children are not "our own," that it is our vocation to be caretakers of our children. "A child is never adopted at the expense of the birthparents, but always in service to them and for the child."[8]

Whose good, then, is chiefly served by adoption? In one clear sense, of course, it is the good of the adopted child. For if children did not need homes and parental nurture, there would be no adoption. But in a deeper sense we can say that, at least when all goes well, the good of all involved is served. That, indeed, should be our aim: that the interests of birth parents, child, and adoptive parents should coincide.

Is the familial bond established by adoption "fictive," an "as if" relationship?

P. D. James's character Philippa Palfrey, whom I quoted above, is clearly no fan of adoption (though she herself was adopted). She eventually learns the identity of her biological mother, who, as it turns out, had murdered a child and been imprisoned for doing so. And she says to her adoptive parents, Maurice and Hilda Palfrey:

> Don't you understand? She's my mother! I can't wipe that out any more than I can wipe out what she did. I can't suddenly learn that she's alive and not want to meet her, get to know her. What do you expect me to do? Go on as if today had never happened? Concoct a new fantasy to live by? Everything you and Hilda have given me is pretense. This is real.[9]

Perhaps Philippa's case is unusual enough that we should not expect to generalize from it, but it seems mistaken to suppose that her life as an adopted child is purely "fantasy" or "pretense." In fact, if anything in her life is real, it is the broken and unhappy relationship between her and her adoptive parents. But she is not the only person to suppose that biology alone is real.

Elizabeth Bartholet, biological mother of one son and adoptive mother of two sons from Peru, recounts how friends of hers would ask of her two adopted sons, who had been raised together in her home, "Are they brothers?" Evidently having been raised for almost their entire lives as her sons did not suffice to make them brothers! Likewise, friends would ask with reference to the son for whom she is biological mother, "How does your *own* child feel about them?" Evidently only he qualified in the full sense as her "own" child.[10] In a similar vein, Russell Moore, also an adoptive parent, writes: "People will often ask me what the key to raising adopted children is. I tell them that honestly, we don't know—we don't have any adopted children. The term 'adopted kid' assumes an ongoing difference, something that differentiates him from a 'regular kid.'"[11]

If we take Bartholet and Moore seriously here, we will not suppose that nothing but biology can form a real familial bond. But we should also be moved to endorse the relatively recent turn toward somewhat greater "openness" in adoption. Though not free of problems, it is, on the whole, wise. I say "on the whole," however, because advocates of openness should be invited to undergo the chastening experience of reading Dietrich Bonhoeffer's short essay, "What Is Meant by 'Telling the Truth'?"[12] As he notes, finding the truthful word is not always easy or obvious. That is because the truth of any particular word cannot be known apart from consideration of the person speaking, the person spoken to, and the setting of their encounter.

> For example, a teacher asks a child in front of the class whether it is true that his father often comes home drunk. It is true, but the child denies it. The teacher's question has placed him in a situation for which he is not yet prepared. He feels only that what is taking place is an unjustified

interference in the order of the family and that he must oppose it. What goes on in the family is not for the ears of the class in school. The family has its own secret and must preserve it. The teacher has failed to respect the reality of this institution. The child ought now to find a way of answering which would comply with both the rule of the family and the rule of the school. But he is not yet able to do this. . . . As a simple no to the teacher's question the child's answer is certainly untrue; yet at the same time it nevertheless gives expression to the truth that the family is an institution *sui generis* and that the teacher had no right to interfere in it. The child's answer can indeed be called a lie; yet this lie contains more truth, that is to say, is more in accordance with reality than would have been the case if the child had betrayed his father's weakness in front of the class. . . . The lies of children, and of inexperienced people in general, are often to be ascribed to the fact that these people are faced with situations which they do not fully understand.[13]

We should not be surprised or upset that adoptive parents may sometimes struggle to find the right way to talk to their children about the circumstances of their adoption. "It is only the cynic who claims 'to speak the truth' at all times and in all places to all men in the same way, but who, in fact, displays nothing but a lifeless image of the truth. He dons the halo of the fanatical devotee of truth who can make no allowance for human weaknesses; but, in fact, he is destroying the living truth between men."[14] There is no one-size-fits-all approach to these questions.

Elizabeth Bartholet has, in fact, noted that the move toward openness in adoption may, paradoxically, disclose a tendency to think of adoption as fictive. On the one hand, those who emphasize the importance of searching for one's birth parents, who argue that adoptees may suffer from "genealogical bewilderment," often seem to doubt that the parent-child bond created by adoption is real. And, on the other hand, those who favor the secrecy of the traditional closed system seem to fear that, if greater openness means that parents and child realize that no biological tie binds them, their relationship will be undermined.[15]

Still, making allowance for such complexities, we should say that, on the whole, the shared life of parents and child should not have its roots in deception. Openness recognizes the fact that some adoptees (more often women than men, it seems)[16] will feel a need to learn the details of their biological origins (and may want or need information for medical purposes). It recognizes that lingering regret of birth parents may be eased if they know the child they gave up for adoption has been nurtured and loved. And it recognizes that adoptive parents not only satisfy their own desire to nurture children but also act in the stead of and in service to the birth parents.

Thus, it is precisely when the bond between adoptive parents and adopted children is rooted in the truth that it takes on the flesh and blood of reality, becoming quite the opposite of any "fictive" or "as if" relationship.

Should single persons adopt? Same-sex couples?
These are clearly different questions; yet in some ways they raise related issues. We can begin by considering whether it is desirable to encourage single persons to adopt. Certainly if a child lacks parents who provide care and nurture, it would be hard to argue that adoption by a single parent would not be in that child's best interests. Even if it would be less desirable than adoption by a husband and wife, there is truth in the common saying that the best can be the enemy of the good. But to say that in a given instance adoption by a single parent may be in the best interests of a child is not to assert that unmarried adults who want children to raise are somehow entitled to them.

Nor does this mean that adoption by a single parent is unproblematic. The important moral questions cannot be dissolved simply by pointing to data which show that an increasingly small percentage of children under eighteen years of age in the United States live with both their mother and father (who are in their first marriage).[17] That information cannot tell us whether this trend is a desirable development. Unlike the case with many married couples who seek to adopt because as a couple they are infertile, adoption by a single parent is not an answer to infertility. (Infertility cannot be a problem of a single individual; it can only afflict a couple.) An unmarried person's decision to adopt may result from a sense of vocation to care for needy children, but it may just as easily result from a sense that anyone who wants a child is entitled to have one. The more attenuated and elastic our concept of a family becomes, the more likely we are to think of children as possessions that help make our life complete and answer to our needs and desires.[18]

There are good reasons to think it is best for children to have both a mother and a father. Some of those reasons are grounded in fairly clear empirical facts—namely, that such families are more likely to provide economic stability and more likely to foster the child's healthy psychological development. Thus, for example, a long article reviewing social scientific studies on the subject offers the carefully qualified thesis that "a broad-based body of theoretical and empirical literature identifies gendered parenting as a key component in a set of influences in shaping children's welfare."[19] While noting many ways in which characteristics exhibited by both mothers and fathers are the primary factors in fostering a child's development, the author also suggests that "the literature clearly supports the perspective that children from families that have well functioning males and females consistently engaged in parenting roles are advantaged because they can see how men and women perform a similar task similarly and differently."[20]

It seems unlikely, however, that empirical studies, which must try to control so many relevant factors, can provide all the clarity we need. It is just as important that we understand the normative significance of complementarity within marriage—the mutual exchange of love between mother and father, modeling for children the power of love to overcome difference.[21] And of all the differences that distinguish us one from another, the sexual difference is surely among the most fundamental. No matter how devoted and capable a single parent may be, he or she cannot provide a sense of the mutual exchange that love involves. Nor, then, can the adopted child be understood as a blessing that is God's yes to the giving and receiving of love between husband and wife.

This means, in my view, that we must regard single parent adoption as a second-best approach. But second best may still be a significant gift for a child who has no stable, permanent place of belonging. It provides that child not just with a place to live—an orphanage or foster care could do that, after all—but with the kind of nurture that only parental commitment can offer. Such arrangements may, to some extent, tempt us to think of a family simply as a voluntary association that satisfies one's desire to have children, but that temptation can be resisted if we focus steadfastly on the best interests of children in need of adoption.

Adoption by same sex parents raises some related and some quite different issues. While those of the same sex may often share deep affection in friendship, Christian tradition has generally held that sexual relations should take place only within the bond of marriage that unites a man and a woman, and only they should form a family. Without arguing the point here, since my focus is on adoption, I will assume the rightness of that traditional Christian view, even though our culture and our law have increasingly turned away from it.[22]

As with single-parent adoption, adoption by parents of the same sex cannot provide for children an image of love that overcomes the difference between women and men. One might, of course, argue that it too should be thought of as a second-best approach, but here the issue is more complicated. A family composed of a single parent and child(ren) runs with the grain of God's creation, even while having about it an air of incompletion. A family composed of a same-sex couple and child(ren) runs counter to the created meaning of the family.

A mother and father are not just "partners." They offer their child different but complementary kinds of care and commitment. Moreover, their married life conforms to the structure God establishes in creation, whereas a same-sex couple sets before a child every day a pattern of life that does not so conform. Consider the dilemma this produces for Christians. If we teach a child of same-sex parents the meaning of marriage as God has created it, we are likely to divide the child's loyalties in a way that even adults might find hard to bear. The child will love, we should hope, those who care for him; the child will also learn to love, we should hope, the way of life to which God calls us. Taken together, these loves may well produce dissonance and tension that are harmful to the child's moral, spiritual, and emotional development.

One of the deep tragedies of our society's increasing ideological commitment to same-sex marriage is that religiously based social service agencies are more and more likely to find themselves forced to choose between agreeing to place children for adoption with same-sex couples and ceasing to provide adoption services altogether. This has already been the case for Roman Catholic agencies at some places in the United States, and the instances of such conflict will almost certainly increase.[23] As that happens, privately arranged adoptions become more frequent. It seems foolish for a society that claims to put first the best interests of children to allow this to happen. That it has happened and is likely to happen more often suggests that we have come to focus less on the best interests of children and more on an adult's supposed entitlement to have a child.

The best response—and for now perhaps the only response—Christians can make to these cultural developments is for the church to find among its members enough married couples and, perhaps, single men or women who are prepared to adopt and provide permanent homes for children who need them. If that is not the case, it will be harder to argue against adoption by same-sex couples.

If an unmarried woman becomes unexpectedly pregnant, should we encourage her to relinquish her child for adoption by a household with both a mother and a father?
This question has too many variants to admit of any single answer. I have already noted that there are good reasons to think it

is best for children to have both a mother and a father. But that need not mean that a single woman who finds herself pregnant should necessarily relinquish her child for adoption if she is able to care for the child. She may have good reasons to do so, and she would not then be wrong to give the child up for adoption, but as we noted earlier, there will be loss involved both for her and for the child.

Sometimes, perhaps often, this question arises when abortion is in view as the alternative to giving up the child for adoption. In that circumstance, adoption is certainly the morally right option. I say that even while realizing how often pregnant women will see the matter in a different light. Four decades of teaching ethics to undergraduates has taught me that many young women, when asked why it would not be better to relinquish their child for adoption than to abort it, will answer that they could not bear the thought of not knowing what had happened to their child.

I confess that this answer leaves me baffled; for, after all, the alternative is that one seeks the death of one's child. But, though baffling, the answer is not unintelligible. A young woman who says this is focusing on the loss she would experience in giving her child to be cared for by others, and there is surely loss involved. Nevertheless, I would want her to think through whether, in imagining herself as a victim here, she has not lost from sight her child who would be the chief victim in abortion. A healthy society should find ways to encourage and support her turn to adoption.

Even if abortion is not in view, it could be that a woman, though old enough to become pregnant, is not old enough to raise a child. Although having a child may seem to give her a kind of standing among her peers, it is not likely to work out well for her future or her child's future—and, again, adoption of the child would be the better option to encourage. But, of course, she may be old enough and mature enough and financially able to raise her child. Were that the case, I would not encourage her to relinquish the child for adoption, nor would I discourage such a decision. We should not set aside natural ties between parents and children in order to engage in a futile search for some optimal family arrangement. Instead, we should try to live faithfully within the created bonds that shape our lives, while acknowledging that sometimes we cannot do so. But in these circumstances our task is not to nudge her in one direction or another but to give her the support she needs to form her own judgment about what is best for her and for her child.

Is it wise for adoption to take place across racial or national boundaries?

How we answer this question—or, at least, the complications involved in any answer we give—will depend on whether we agree with Martha Nussbaum, who, characterizing a Stoic vision with which she seems to concur, writes, "The accident of where one is born is just that, an accident; any human being might have been born in any nation."[24] I suspect that we will want both to agree and to disagree. On the one hand, we want to affirm the one human family in which each of us shares an equal dignity. "God created man," Augustine writes, "as one individual; but that did not mean that he was to remain alone, bereft of human society. God's intention was that in this way the unity of human society and the bonds of human sympathy be more emphatically brought home to man, if men were bound together not merely by likeness in nature but also by the feeling of kinship."[25] And that, surely, seems right.

On the other hand, unless we think of human beings as pure spirits untouched by time and place, it would be foolish to suppose that it makes no difference at all to my identity if I am born in Chicago or in Tuscaloosa—or Prague or Damascus. No one is just a citizen of the world. Yet, Nussbaum insists that to treat national boundaries as if they were "morally salient" is to give to "an accident of history a false air of moral weight."[26]

Were we to be convinced by her position, a clear answer to the question about the significance of national boundaries—and probably also racial boundaries—would seem to follow. They may perhaps enrich life in some ways, but they could hardly be permitted to stand in the way when the needs of children call for adoption. I doubt, however, that we should find Nussbaum's sort of cosmopolitanism convincing. Although the "accidents" of birth, of time and place, do not carry ultimate moral significance, neither are they unimportant for shaping personal identity and forming our life in community.

Of course, international adoption did not arise as the answer to a philosophical conundrum. Although the practice of adoption itself goes back centuries, the widespread practice in the United States of international adoption "grew out of orphan-rescue missions in the wake of military conflicts"—World War II, the Korean War, and the Vietnam War.[27] Thus, for example, more than 110,000 South Korean children are estimated to have been adopted in the United States between 1955 and 2001, a number that is "approximately 10% of the present-day Korean American population."[28] No doubt the motives of those promoting adoption across national borders were mixed—from "a new superpower's desire to demonstrate its good will to the rest of the world" to a belief "that love could transcend any cultural barrier."[29] But even our best motives are generally mixed. If actions that are right and praiseworthy could not proceed from mixed motives, few of us could ever claim to act rightly.

To be sure, the philosophical problem will never go away. Because it is possible to think of a person's identity either as deeply *embedded* in a particular cultural context or as *threatened* by the way in which such a context may undermine one's individuality—and because, in fact, there is some truth in each of these perspectives—it is no surprise that adoption across national borders has been controversial. On the one hand, there are times when the need for it is compelling, "a remarkable experiment in human kinship, flaws and all," as John Seabrook described it in an account of his family's adoption of a young Haitian girl after the earthquake of January 2010.[30] On the other hand, at times, at least in the eyes of some, it is less a rescue operation than baby snatching by the rich and powerful (who desire children) at the expense of the poor and vulnerable (birth mothers in particular)—or, put more politically, a new form of colonialism.[31] That there have been instances of serious abuse seems evident, but, whatever the problems with international adoption, it does respond to a clear need.

People understand the term "orphan" in a variety of ways, but, at a minimum, there are almost 18 million orphans worldwide—children who have lost both parents and are living in orphanages or on the streets.[32] As recently as 2013 just under eight thousand children were adopted from other countries by citizens of the United States, a number that does little more than scratch the surface of the need.[33] How our law might best respond to this continuing need is disputed and is not easy to determine, but the seriousness of the need should not be denied.[34] In principle, therefore, we should approve those who cross boundaries of nation and culture to adopt children in need. We might, in fact, think of these families, "whose members must learn to appreciate one another's differences while experiencing their common humanity," as living out in practice a response to a philosophical tension for which we are not likely ever to find a perfect theoretical solution.[35]

Because we give credence to each of two political commitments that stand in some tension, our society will continue to have difficulty resolving the issues raised by adoption across national borders. On the one hand, we believe in individual autonomy and do not think a person's identity is determined or defined entirely by his social location. On the other hand, we pay homage to the idea of multiculturalism, believing that our identity may be determined less by belonging to the one human family than by membership in more narrowly defined cultural groups, which shape and even constitute us as the people we are.

Because the first of these commitments, though sometimes overstated, is not entirely mistaken, international adoption cannot fairly be characterized simply as cultural exploitation. Neither, however, should we be surprised if it sometimes seems problematic. For, although we share membership in the human family, the second commitment is also not entirely mistaken. The identity of each of us has been shaped in distinctive ways by the time and place we inhabit. For Christians these "accidents" of time and place are the work of the Creator and can never be unimportant, but neither can they have the final word about a person's identity. In the end, we are called toward a community in which each can know the other as "brother" or "sister," and, even if that calling cannot be fully realized here and now, it must help to form and direct our practice.

Adoption across racial boundaries raises similar questions. Because of the long history in the United States first of slavery and segregation, and then of continuing racial tension, it also presents special problems. Like intercountry adoption, transracial adoption in the United States is largely a development that followed World War II. The number of such adoptions was growing rapidly until 1972, when the National Association of Black Social Workers took the position that black children should be placed for adoption only in black families. Only then, so the argument went, could these children form a strong and healthy sense of their identity as black people.[36]

At least in principle, however, federal law—in the Multiethnic Placement Act of 1994 as amended in 1996 by legislation on Removal of Barriers to Interethnic Adoption—has been intended to encourage adoption across racial boundaries. It prohibits delaying or denying placement of a child for adoption on the basis of the race of the child or adoptive parent(s). But, of course, federal legislation governs only state agencies that receive federal funds and does not control the practice of private adoption agencies.

The deeper conceptual issues raised by transracial adoption are similar to those taken up above in connection with international adoption. A person's identity is deeply shaped by his time, place, and ancestry. But those factors can also undermine individual identity if they cause us to overlook or deny our common humanity. One way, quite popular in recent decades, of dealing with race in our still race-conscious society has been to argue that the concept of race itself is merely a social construct with no basis in biology or genetics. So, for example, mapping of the human genome has demonstrated that people of all races share more than 99.99% of their genetic material. Nonetheless, as Armand Marie Leroi has noted, our increasing knowledge of molecular biology is likely to show that the attempt to undercut the very concept of race has been taken further than the evidence warrants.[37]

Leroi points to ways in which recognition of racial differences is important for medical care. But at least as important for our concern here is his suggestion that the need to recognize race "does not rest on purely utilitarian grounds. There is also an aesthetic factor. We are a physically variable species." The more seriously we take that, the more inclined we will be to admit the importance of race for shaping one's sense of self—and, hence, its significance for shaping our adoption practices.

But this cannot, I think, be the last word, for no person belongs to any (racial or national) community to the whole extent of his being. Those distinctions do not obliterate the kinship we all share. And therefore, given the continued need of many children for a home in which they truly belong, Paul Lauritzen is surely correct to argue that putting their interests first "would lead to active endorsement of transracial adoption, particularly when the alternatives are foster care or institutionalization."[38] How much more so, then, for Christians, who have been taught and who believe that flesh and blood will not inherit the kingdom God promises.

Interlude III
Being Adopted

Dear Derek:

I've written you several letters already, and it occurs to me that, although I've talked about how we adopted you, I haven't said all that much about what being adopted actually means. We should think together about this before I finish these letters.

It's natural, I think, that you should wonder about that—about why you're adopted, whether it makes any difference, and whether it makes you a different sort of person. Obviously, we don't plan or intend that children should be adopted. We expect that children can be cared for by their biological parents, and usually they are. That's a good thing. Those biological ties are important, because human beings are bodies. We're connected to each other by bonds of kinship and descent, in which a child is a kind of bodily image of the marriage of a man and woman. If we pretended this was not important, we'd be thinking of ourselves as more like angels—bodiless spirits. But we're not made like that.

Children are a gift God gives parents, and usually this gift turns out to help both parents and children. Parents begin to

65

learn what it means really to love and care for someone else. They learn that their own plans and desires must often be interrupted or even set aside because of the needs of their children. And children learn what it means to have someone love them unconditionally—not because they have certain abilities or talents, but just because parents love their children.

Sometimes this doesn't work out, though. Then we have to remember that we are not just bodies who have to accept whatever happens, but are also free to step in and try to help when things go wrong. That's what adoption is for, and that's why you are adopted. Your parents just couldn't take care of you, and so you needed to be taken into another home where you could have a mother and a father. You needed to have parents who could and would love you unconditionally, for without that kind of love no child can flourish (as, indeed, you have flourished).

So the "natural" connection of parents and children is important, but human beings are not only "natural" but also "historical" beings. I was not your biological father, but after you'd been living with us for a few years—after we'd shared that much history—I had nevertheless become your true father.

How long does that take? Who can say? Probably it dawns upon us only gradually that it is happening or has happened. But at some point it became clear to Mom and me that—without any biological connection at all—you had nevertheless become our son, and we had become your parents. This too is a gift God gives, even if it's not given in the natural, biological way. So adoption goes beyond biology—but also mimics it. When you were adopted you were given not just two people who would care for you, but a new mother and father, from whom you yourself could gradually learn what it means to be part of a family.

Does it make any difference that you're adopted? Well, of course, it does. How could it not? It means you have a special history that's a little different from that of many other people. It means, I hope, that as you grow older you will appreciate just how important is the bond of parents with their children and will be able to help others appreciate it as well. And certainly I hope you'll know—with an absolute certainty—that you have received love without condition and are therefore now able to give such love as well.

This is finally a theological point, and I think I'll need one more letter to do it justice. That'll give you something to look forward to!

Love,

Dad

(*Christian Century*, August 23, 2003)

CHAPTER 4

Assisted Reproduction and Adoption

Here's a puzzle: If we approve of forming families via adoption, families not grounded in biological ties, why not also approve assisted reproduction using donated sperm or ova? And if we disapprove those reproductive technologies, can we still coherently support adoption? My aim in this chapter is to think through that puzzle and try to make sense of the following claim: Christians should be strong supporters of adoption (which one can do while acknowledging that there are abuses in the practice of adoption, as there are in any large scale social practice), but, for the most part, they should not make use of new reproductive technologies.

I have not dreamed up this puzzle. Once we start to think about the practice of adoption, we are likely to ask ourselves: If we say no to assisted reproduction, should we not also say no to adoption? Or, in Timothy Jackson's fuller formulation: "At its best, adoption is motivated by the desire to care for and educate children, but it might seem to be a problematic case of acquiring offspring without having had sex. If the Roman Catholic Church forbids artificial means of conception, why does it permit adoption?"[1] And, as I noted, we can make the same point by reversing the form of the question: If we have said yes to adoption, should we not also say yes to various forms of assisted reproduction? Ted Peters puts the argument that way: "If what we think of as the traditional family can spread its apron to enclose families with adopted children, families with surrogate children should also be considered traditional."[2] The puzzle is a simple one. If the lack of a biological tie counts so much in the one instance—counts enough to give us reason to oppose at least some forms of assisted reproduction—why should its absence not also count against adoption? By plunging ahead with various forms of assisted reproduction without thinking through their full implications, our society has brought such questions upon itself. We cannot avoid thinking about them.

On Forming a Family

It is all too easy to think of adoption and assisted reproduction as two ways of doing essentially the same thing—acquiring a child to rear. It is important at the outset to be clear about why we should not think this. In the mutual exchange of gifts between adoptive parents and children, the parents' desire to raise children and form a family is served, but the satisfaction of their desire should never be the chief justification for the practice of adoption. Although adoption is, to be sure, motivated in part by the desire to care for children, it is not, at least in Christian eyes, a method of "acquiring" children. They do not become our possessions any more than do children who are biologically ours. At its best, the desire and need of would-be parents should coincide with the desire and need of children for a family to which they belong. Thus, children are not produced *in order* to be available for adoption; they are available for adoption because those who produced them are unable or unwilling to care for them. Then the needs of the child, the needs of birth parents, and the needs of potential adoptive parents meet and are mutually served. If we think about adoption in that way, we will not suppose that assisted reproduction and adoption are simply two different ways of doing the same thing—namely, acquiring a child to rear.

Of course, we live in a world in which assisted reproduction is not a rare occurrence, and its increasing hold on our culture tempts some to rethink the meaning of adoption. For example, John Robertson, well known as a knowledgeable advocate of new reproductive technologies, suggests that our increasing acceptance of assisted reproduction will eventually "loop back" to adoption and "undermine the foundations of adoption law."[3] What he has in mind is this: as we permit—and, even, endorse a right of—people to engage in collaborative reproduction using gamete donors and gestational surrogates, what makes someone a parent seems to be the *intention* to acquire and rear a child. It gets harder and harder to argue that one's genetic connection to a child has any moral significance unless we intend that it should. (Indeed, it gets harder and harder to maintain the biological paradigm at all. Robertson does not speak of "parents" but of "partners." A vestige of tradition remains in his regular use of the word "couple," but that lingering aspect of tradition will not long survive.)

How does acceptance of assisted reproduction "loop back" to and undermine our practice of adoption? Given that a "couple" seeking a child to rear might commission others to serve as gamete donors and as gestational surrogate, yet consider themselves that child's parents because they have orchestrated the project, we might reasonably conclude that "preconception rearing intentions should count as much as or more than biologic connection."[4] But, of course, our current adoption law does not permit preconception contracts to produce children for adoption. In Robertson's view, this seeming incoherence cannot long survive, nor indeed should it if adoption is simply another way of acquiring a child without having sex. "In the end," Robertson hypothesizes, "we may come to accept paid, commissioned pregnancies in carefully defined circumstances as another avenue for infertile couples seeking to form a family."[5]

This prediction misses entirely the distinction I noted above. It is premised on the notion that those who commission an assisted reproduction project and those who undertake to adopt are *doing* essentially the same thing. But they are not. The *result* in each case may look similar—parents with a child to raise. What they *do*, however, and the practices in which they engage are very different.

No doubt Robertson's prediction (or is it a recommendation?) is supposed to be saved from complete insouciance by the words "in carefully defined circumstances." But those words are inadequate to guard against the practice Robertson seems willing to contemplate. For, after all, what he is suggesting is that our society might endorse a practice in which some people beget a child in order to meet the needs and desires of other would-be parents. Even if these "commissioned" pregnancies were not in every instance "paid," the children begotten would still be thought of and treated as property that could be given by one person to another. Before we consider any "loop back" to adoption, we need to be clear about the moral meaning of gamete donation.

For the moment we should probably say that our culture is simply confused, its approach to such donation lacking coherence. On the one hand, we seem to think that the intention to rear a child produced with others' gametes, and the commissioning of such a project, is sufficient to make one a parent. But, on the other hand, our culture has also produced the Human Genome Project, and it has reinforced in many people's minds the unfortunate notion that scientific information about our genes is, at the same time, information about our kinship relations.[6] If, however, close genetic connection is what makes us kin, an infertile couple's use of gamete donation would seem to disrupt rather than extend their kinship bond. Hence, Kaja Finkler writes, "The new genetics frames a vision of kinship that conflicts with contemporary notions of choosing one's family and kin independent of reproduction and blood ties."[7]

Exploring this notion, Finkler interviewed a number of adoptees who had searched for their birth mother. (They are, we should note, the exception, since the majority of adoptees do not search.)[8] How much we can generalize from such a study is hard to say, of course, but Finkler's own conclusion is that most of those who searched thought of their identity in rather passive terms. That is, they thought of themselves as people "whose interests and personalities are transmitted entirely genetically, rather than acquired by experience and by their own abilities to interpret the world around them."[9] Many of us, it seems, have come to know just enough about genetics to think of ourselves in that way—as "a passive container" shaped by our genes.[10]

In short, our society's concept of a family is at odds with itself. On the one hand, we sometimes think of a family as people who, bound together by affective ties, have chosen to share a common household. This way of thinking may have some features in common with the practice of adoption, although it need not include the central purpose of adoption—namely, to provide a place of belonging for a child who needs a home. Such a concept of the family as an intentional, chosen bond has, of course, become especially prominent in our public disagreements about the issue of same-sex marriage, but in some respects it is well suited to the world of assisted reproduction. For in that world preconception intentions are thought by many to be the crucial factor establishing parenthood. In other respects, however, making preconception intentions so important clashes with the way we talk about new reproductive technologies. For, after all, if it is simply shared love and the decision to form a common household that make a family, we may have a hard time explaining why infertile couples should want "a child of their own," a child who has some genetic relation to at least one of them. That should not matter in a world where parent-child bonds are more a result of intention and choice than of genetic connection.

Where should the emphasis lie? On the intention and choice to be a parent? Or on the genes that make one person a direct genetic progenitor of another? The practice of assisted reproduction seems to want both. So, for example, we now commonly talk about the possibility that a child might have as many as five "parents"—two who commission the reproductive project, two who donate gametes, and one who gestates. In truth, however, this is less a clarification than an admission that we do not know how to name the human connections we have created. Once we sever all connection between the two goods—relational and procreative—of marriage, once the begetting of children is no longer thought of as the natural fruition of the mutual love of husband and wife, we enter a world in which it is hard not to think of children as products we produce to satisfy our desires and may convey to others to satisfy theirs. Christian thinkers, too, may struggle to fashion a coherent perspective.

A TROUBLING ARGUMENT

In criticizing—rightly—our culture's increasing acceptance of assisted reproduction and its abrupt endorsement of same-sex partners (who may use assisted reproduction to acquire children), Christian thinkers can all too readily turn to arguments that not only oppose those practices but may also seem to undermine the practice of adoption. If that happens, we should be clear that something has gone wrong with the argument.

Thus, for example, Gerard Bradley constructs an argument designed to indicate why two people of the same sex cannot establish a form of life that we should call a family.[11] His argument begins from a premise that is, at least in my view, correct. When a husband and wife engage in sexual relations and their mutual self-giving is blessed with the gift of a child, that child—along with any other children they may have—is a visible manifestation of their one-flesh union. The child they beget is not a reproductive project or the product of whatever preconception intentions they may have shared. Even if they fervently hoped for a child, their children are, as Bradley puts it in rather technical language, "gifts that supervene upon the spouses' marital act." Husband and wife give themselves in love to each other, and their mutual self-giving is blessed with a child. The presence of a child may make the parents very happy, but the child is not a product "called forth 'intentionally' to satisfy the parents' desires, objectives, or needs." Hence, it makes sense to think of the child as a gift or blessing.[12]

Still more, because they are not intentionally produced to satisfy desires, the children of these parents are equal in dignity to their parents and to each other. "All the children are equally and wholly the offspring of the same parents; mother and father are equally and wholly parents of each child, in whom they see (literally) so many unique, yet related and, in a sense, identical expressions of their own union."[13]

So far, so good. But what then shall we think about the following two sentences, in which Bradley attempts to nail down the argument? "The lifelong and unbreakable cords of fealty and identity that family members possess for each other, and which even distance and alienation never quite erase, depend on this biological matrix. No other 'family' form can replace it."[14] What exactly does this mean for families formed by adoption? In his concern to demonstrate the problem with families formed by assisted reproduction (in some instances used by same-sex couples), Bradley has done more than he (or, at least, we) might have bargained for. He has constructed an argument that seems to assign adoptive families to permanent second-class status.

If, as I noted earlier in chapter 2, adoption is actually the very heart of the New Testament, can this possibly be satisfactory? Put in the terms that earlier chapter drew from Karl Barth, Bradley's argument isolates one moment in the history of redemption, that of God's work in creation, and takes it as entirely sufficient for understanding the nature of the family. But God's work of reconciliation, which teaches that we are children of God not by nature but by grace, must also shape our vision. Indeed, as Jeanne Stevenson-Moessner puts it, the genealogy of Jesus in Matthew's Gospel, by naming Joseph as Jesus' adoptive father and thereby creating a discontinuity in Jesus' biological line, "alter[s] the biologic flow of lineage and inaugurate[s] the Christian era."[15]

The natural bond formed by our biological connections is important, and it teaches us, as Bradley nicely unfolds, what it means to think of children as gifts or to affirm the equal dignity of children with each other and with their parents. We can even find a way to say, as he does, that no other family form can entirely replace that created form. For, as much as possible we should want the structure of families formed by adoption to be patterned after God's work in creation—that is, to join wife, husband, and children in the bond of familial belonging.

As the work of God in creation the natural family should be honored and affirmed. Alongside it, however, and just as deserving of our affirmation and honor, are families patterned after it but formed through adoption and the shared history adoption produces. That history can help to heal the wound our fallen nature inflicts on natural life, and it provides for children a place of belonging that—in their case—biology has failed to provide. "You are indeed designed," Russell Moore writes, "to love 'your own flesh and blood,' but your design is redeemed in Christ to see as your flesh and blood those whom you previously didn't recognize as such."[16] We should not construct arguments that undermine this central Christian insight. What we want, as Moore says, is to be parents, not simply "conservators" of our "genetic material."[17]

Do Genes Make the Parent?

As I noted earlier, there is something quite confusing about the way many have come to think about the new reproductive technologies. People who are eager—perhaps, even, desperate—to have "a child of their own" use sperm or ova donated by others.[18] Then, lacking a genetic connection to the child they have produced and intend to rear, they must decide whether to keep secret their use of donated gametes or to openly acknowledge that others participated in their reproductive project. And, at least at first sight, this question might seem similar to ongoing debates about whether adoption should be open or closed. To think of these as related questions would mean, however, that we think of gamete donors as analogous to parents who have relinquished their child for adoption—an unconvincing analogy. After all, no child whom a gamete donor might relinquish yet exists.

Nevertheless, we have come to speak of and distinguish genetic parents, rearing (or social, or commissioning) parents, and a gestational (surrogate) parent. As I noted earlier, however, this language is less a clarification than it is simply an admission that we do not really know how to describe the "familial" bonds we have created. Having separated the production of children from the sexual relation between spouses, we do not know how to put this broken world together again.

When a child is adopted, the adoptive parents act on behalf of the biological parents, providing for their child a place of belonging that the parents who were the procreators—who conceived, gestated, and perhaps reared the child for a time—cannot provide. As Elizabeth Kirk puts it, adopting a child is not done "at the expense of the birthparents, but always in service to them and for the child."[19] Adoptive parents have not procreated; rather, they act in a way that "can only be described adequately as charity—a coming to the aid of natural parents."[20] It seems right, therefore, that adopted children should, if they wish, know something of the parents who gave them birth. Others now act in the stead of those birth parents, but not by eliminating them entirely from their child's history.

By contrast, parents who use assisted reproduction technologies are not acting in the place of or on behalf of those who provide sperm or ova. If anything, the opposite is true. Gamete donors provide a kind of assistance that commissioners of a reproductive project need to bring it to completion. Whereas adoptive parents act in service to birth parents and an already existing child, gamete donors simply provide something that is needed for the success of someone else's reproductive project. The child produced by that project has not been shaped by any shared history with the gamete donors. This is not to argue for donor anonymity; it is simply to recognize the enormous gulf that separates adoption from assisted reproduction using donated gametes. "To take another's child into one's family is a totally different kind of act from taking another's gamete into one's act of procreation."[21]

The more we clarify for ourselves what adoption actually means (or should mean), and the more we appreciate the significance it has for Christians who know themselves to be adopted children of Jesus's Father, the less inclined we should be to rest the full weight of parenthood on genetic or biological connection. Quite perceptively Michael Banner has compared *Donum Vitae: Instruction on Respect for Human Life in Its Origin and on the Dignity of Procreation*, issued in 1987 by the Roman Catholic Congregation for the Doctrine of the Faith,[22] with the Warnock Report, issued in 1984 in the United Kingdom by the Committee of Inquiry into Human Fertilisation and Embryology. Banner observes that these two perspectives, at first sight seemingly so opposed, actually try to "outbid" each other in expressing "profound respect for biological parenthood."[23] Of course, *Donum Vitae* does so in order to reject techniques of assisted reproduction. The Warnock Report does so in order to approve such techniques as an aid to infertile couples.

Banner suggests, however, that we might regard their different verdicts on reproductive technologies as "a relatively minor disagreement between parties which share very similar understandings of the relationship between parent and child."[24] And, although he by no means endorses the conclusions of the Warnock Report, there is a sense in which he faults *Donum Vitae* still more. For what it does, he argues, is leave infertile couples "in a double bind—they are forbidden to make use of technologies that might assist them in realizing their desire for parenthood, fully biological or otherwise, while that desire is left solemnly in place on its contemporary pedestal."[25] Banner, by contrast, wants to underscore the New Testament affirmation that we are children of Jesus's Father by adoption, by grace rather than nature, and that this truth must underlie our understanding of the bond that joins parents with their children.

There are moments when, at least in my judgment, Banner comes close to overstating his case. Thus, for example, he says that Christianity does not think it a "tragedy" to be childless, and that "Christians do not believe in the desperateness of childlessness."[26] The first of these claims seems to me to diminish unnecessarily the work of God in creation by which a husband and wife quite naturally anticipate and desire children who are a blessing upon their mutual self-giving. The second, though, seems right. Infertility should not be experienced as "desperate" by Christians, for in the new covenant inaugurated by Jesus, a covenant made ours by adoption, our children—however close and certain their biological attachment to us—are never simply "ours." We do not bend the knee before the blood tie.

Two Kinds of Family History

Quite a few years ago, when I was teaching at Oberlin College, Jaroslav Pelikan, the noted church historian and student of many languages, came to speak at the college. I was among a small group that went to dinner with him, and he immediately sought to explore the origins of my (clearly German) surname. From where had my ancestors come to this country? When? What details could I give him?

At the time it was a little embarrassing for me to have to admit that I had no idea how to answer his questions. I had simply never cared enough about it to explore such questions with my father or grandfather. No doubt my ancestry had marked and shaped me in certain ways, but I had little interest in reflecting upon those ways, whatever they might be. Moreover, I confess that to this day I do not regard that lack of interest as a defect, but we can think about it in light of a fascinating paper by the philosopher David Velleman entitled "Family History."[27]

Velleman begins by observing what is true of all of us. We are heirs of a "biological" ancestry, and we also have a "cultural" inheritance given us by those who rear us. The question he asks is: Does it matter if these two inheritances are not the same? Does it matter if those who raise us are not our biological ancestors?[28] Velleman thinks it does matter in important ways. He writes to explain why and to oppose what he calls a "new ideology of the family" (360) that thinks it does not. Because Velleman disagrees with that ideology, the thrust of his argument is to oppose all use of donor gametes in assisted reproduction. For the moment, however, I am less concerned with that conclusion than with his discussion of the importance of family history.

In making the case for the importance of knowing one's biological ancestors, Velleman points to the fact that some adopted children search for their birth parents. When they do, he says, "there is a literal sense in which they are searching for themselves" (368). They have been deprived of something that is very important to human beings. That is no fault of their own, of course, nor does Velleman offer it as a reason for objecting to adoption. After all, if a child already exists, a child whose biological parents are unable or unwilling to care for him, it is good that this child should be provided a home through adoption. Still, the child has suffered a loss, and Velleman describes that loss in very strong terms. "Not knowing any biological relatives must be like wandering in a world without reflective surfaces, permanently self-blind" (368).

That strikes me as much too strong a claim, whatever element of truth it may contain. Velleman argues that we come to know ourselves and our possibilities in large part through family resemblance. Forming a "concept of myself" would, he thinks, "be very difficult were I not acquainted with people to whom I bear a literal family resemblance" (366). Getting to know my biological relatives helps me know what sort of person I am. And getting to know the history of my biological relatives helps me have a sense of what it means to be this sort of person, what my possibilities may be. Rather than trying to imagine what sort of person I am by seeing myself as others see me, I can simply look at my parents, my siblings, and other close relatives in order to learn a great deal about who I am.

Perhaps there is no definitive way to prove or disprove these claims, but I myself do not find them persuasive. For one thing, children in a family, sharing biological parents and family history, can nonetheless be very different sorts of people. Indeed, that is one of the great gifts of exogamous marriage; it extends the boundaries of human friendship, as Thomas Aquinas so nicely put it.[29] We are invited and compelled to live daily with those who may be very different from us, and to learn to love and care for them. Moreover, Velleman's belief that family history relieves me of the need to try to know myself by seeing how others see me overlooks the important claim—as old as Aristotle—that the friend provides "another self," one who reflects back to me the person I really am, and without whom I can hardly attain self-fulfillment.

None of this means that Velleman is mistaken to oppose the use of donated gametes. He is quite right to note that, whereas adoption is chiefly about doing something for a child in need (while also serving the parental desires of the adopting parents), using donated gametes to produce a child is chiefly about would-be parents doing something for themselves. Velleman notes that those who commission such a reproductive project generally acquire a child who has at least some biological relation to them. And on Velleman's terms, of course, they are getting something good for themselves, since that biological relation is good. They gain this, however, precisely by frustrating the child's needs—on Velleman's terms—for that very same good. "I regard this as morally incoherent," he writes (374). It would be hard to deny the incoherence. For even if we are not prepared—as I am not—to make biological family history as important for identity as Velleman supposes, the point is that those who commission such reproductive projects do seem to think it very important. And thinking that, they nevertheless deprive the child of the good they gain for themselves.

It remains to take stock of where we find ourselves. I have argued that those who adopt and those who use new reproductive technologies are not *doing* the same thing. Hence, endorsing adoption need not commit us to endorsing those technologies. But *may* we endorse them even if we *need* not? That adopted children lack a genetic connection with their parents does not, in my view, give Christians any reason to draw back from or question the worth of the practice of adoption. (And we can say this without denying the significance of genetic connection; for it is part of the ordered world God has created.) But if lack of genetic connection is no reason to question the worth of adoption, it might seem to follow that the use of donated gametes or a surrogate in assisted reproduction, which also severs the genetic connection between the child and one or both parents, is no reason to question the use of new reproductive technologies.

What, if any, reasons might we still have, then, for questioning the use of donated gametes in assisted reproduction projects? There are, I think, two reasons for concern—one having to do with implications for the dignity of the child produced, the other with implications for the marital union of husband and wife.

A child conceived by means of assisted reproduction technologies that use donated sperm or ova is not simply a blessing bestowed upon the giving and receiving of love by a husband and wife, God's "yes" to their mutual self-giving. The child becomes something other than just the object of their hope or desire. Instead the child is a product, the result of a project they have undertaken (and for which they have commissioned the assistance of others). Of course this does not mean that children conceived in such a way will not be loved. Not at all. Those who have commissioned the project precisely in order to have a child whom they can raise are likely to be delighted to have that child. But a society that allows itself to begin to think of children in this way is one that, over time, may find it difficult to affirm the equal dignity of all its members. For, after all, some of them exist to satisfy the desires of others.

The use of gametes provided by third parties is troubling not only because the desired child becomes a product but also because of what it might mean for the relation of the spouses. A third party may now seem to be present in their procreative act. There is, of course, an obvious way to deny that. We may simply suggest, reasonably enough, that the donor should remain anonymous and the fact that donated gametes have been used should be concealed. (To be sure, it cannot be concealed from the spouses themselves, and the psychic impact upon their marriage of that shared, secret knowledge might be hard to calculate.) On this view only sperm and ova—not the providers of those materials—are present in the couple's procreation. To the degree that this is psychologically possible, it provides a way to avoid supposing that others are personally present in the procreative act of the spouses, and it suggests a reason to favor anonymity of gamete donors. Indeed, if our society permits gamete donation, it would be wise to make clear that supplying gametes is not itself a procreative act and does not make one a parent.

Nevertheless, an increasingly large number of people seem to find that hard to believe. Many now reject the idea that gamete donors should remain anonymous, arguing that a parental relation (of some sort) is established between those who provide gametes and the child who results. But this means, we should then admit, that the gamete provider remains personally present in the act of procreation and cannot disappear from the familial picture. And that, as Oliver O'Donovan has observed, forces us to ask, "How can the third party be personally present in the act of begetting, without being intrusive into the relationship from which the begetting springs?"[30]

Thus, for several related reasons that have no inherent connection to adoption, assisted reproduction with donated gametes is problematic. It invites us to think of children as products, perhaps even products produced to meet our specifications. It invites us to think of our marriages in ways that cannot see children as blessings bestowed upon our mutual self-giving in love. And, even when as individuals we resist such invitations, it forms a culture whose understanding of these fundamental human relationships is almost inevitably distorted. Hence, Christians who oppose gamete donation and surrogacy have no need to construct their arguments in ways that could undermine the practice of adoption.

Let us linger here for a moment to underscore once again why those who adopt do something quite different from what is done by those who make use of new reproductive technologies. To become parents through open adoption, acknowledging the existence and identity of the adopted child's birth parents, does not intrude any third party into the procreative life of the couple who adopt. They have not procreated, they have adopted—taking a child into their family in service to that child, to the child's birth parents, and (almost certainly) to their own desire to nurture and rear children. Even if they are infertile, and their lovemaking has not proved to be life-giving, no third party has been used in an attempt to make their shared love fruitful.

What of those instances in which assisted reproduction makes use of no third parties, whether gamete providers or a surrogate? A married couple may have an embryo formed in vitro using their own sperm and ovum, then implanted in the wife's womb to gestate and bring to birth. That calls for a somewhat more nuanced evaluation.

There are, I think, occasions in the moral life when we may not want to say that an action is wrong, even though we may also be reluctant to encourage it and inclined to discourage it. Something like that, I think, is the case here. After all, the embryo will be externalized in assisted reproduction, available in the laboratory for inspection and analysis. It may be harder for the prospective parents not to think of their hoped-for child as a product, harder not to want to produce the best possible child—harder, that is, to resist eugenic temptations.

Once we think about it, we will see that the language of "assisted" reproduction may be slightly misleading. We are not just assisting a husband and wife to procreate, whatever exactly it would mean to assist in that undertaking. We are doing something a little different, something that engages our capacity for will and choice before it engages our bodies and their passions. Once we decide to produce a child, it will be hard not to commit ourselves to producing the best child possible. This is already clearly the case with the increasingly frequent use of preimplantation genetic diagnosis, in which embryos produced in vitro are screened and either accepted for implantation or rejected. Indeed, some might even argue that it would be irresponsible not to screen, that those who decide to produce a product are responsible for exercising some quality control. To be sure, those eugenic temptations can be resisted, but doing so will require standing firm against a kind of momentum that takes over once the process has begun. Acknowledging these dangers, we can see why it might be morally better never to set foot on this path.

One last concern, different from eugenic temptations, should be noted. Built into the use of reproductive technologies, even when no third parties are involved, may be the production of more embryos than are needed at any one time. This is not absolutely necessary, since it would be possible to implant all embryos produced and to produce only as many as we are willing to implant. That makes the process more difficult, however, and it is no surprise that we now have frozen hundreds of thousands of (what are called in a very unfortunate locution) "spare" embryos. We should never have set foot on a path that leads to such an end, but we have. What to do about it is a problem to be taken up in the next chapter.

Interlude IV
Adoptees One and All

Dear Derek:

I wrote last time that being adopted makes you different, and so it does. But I also hinted that we still had one more thing to think about in order really to get the proper theological perspective on adoption.

Has it occurred to you that every Christian is adopted? That's what St. Paul says in Galatians chapter 4. God sent his Son Jesus, Paul writes, "so that we might receive adoption as sons." And because we have become God's children by adoption, he has "sent the Spirit of his Son into our hearts, crying, 'Abba! Father!'" Each one of us has been rescued from our natural state; each has experienced the love of a new and better father; each has become part of a new and better family. So you might think of your own experience of being adopted as an image—inadequate and hazy, to be sure—of what each of us can and must experience if we are really to flourish as human beings made to know the love of God. By God's grace, we're all adoptees.

Once we see this, we should realize that there's a sense in which every Christian father or mother is, in some respects, an adoptive parent—even of their own biological children. Think, for instance, of what we believe happens in baptism. Parents hand their child over to God in baptism, and the child becomes part of that new family, the body of Christ. In other words, parents acknowledge that, important and dear to us as our families are, it is even more important to be taken by adoption into that new family in which we learn to name as our Father the One whom Jesus called his Father. So we relinquish our children and then receive them back—not as our possession but as those God gives us to care for.

This, by the way, is why it's such a mistake when—as sometimes happens—Christians begin to think of baptism as primarily a family event. It's only natural, of course, that family members take special interest in the occasion. But if we begin to think of it as an event primarily for them, it's almost as if we're missing what baptism is really about for Christian faith. We're treating as essential what baptism itself teaches us is not the most important thing.

I think, in fact, that having you for a son has taught me this more clearly than years of theological study. If someone had asked me twenty years ago whether I could love a child who was not my biological child as much as one who was, I would have said that I doubted it. The biological tie seemed so important— and is so important—that I just couldn't imagine that the lack of it could be overcome. You have taught me that I was wrong, for I know that I love you every bit as much as Peter, Ellen, or Hannah. So, thanks to you, I've learned something about myself.

But more important, I've learned a crucial theological lesson. We might say that biological parents are, in a way, obligated to love their children, while adoptive parents do not act from obligation. There's something to that, and—precisely because there is—we should remember that God is under no obligation to love us and does not love us because he must.

Why, then, does he love us? Well, how can I answer that question except with another? Why do I love you? Just because I do.

And—likewise—just because God does. We have no claims on God. We cannot plead the importance of biological kinship. We can only learn to be grateful that, for his own mysterious reasons, he has adopted us as his children.

I like to think that this is a lesson you will not forget. It will, I think, make you yourself a better father some day. I hope I'm around to see that day, because I have every confidence that you'll be a good one.

Love,
Dad
(*Christian Century*, September 6, 2003)

CHAPTER 5

Adopting Embryos

There are in the United States hundreds of thousands of frozen embryos, most of them produced for but then not used in attempts to conceive with the aid of assisted reproduction technologies.[1] What to do with them is a question in search of an answer, and there does not seem to be any very good answer.

We could leave them in limbo, frozen indefinitely and to some degree forgotten. No doubt they would eventually degrade, though it is hard to say how long "eventually" would be. Nor is it clear that a decision thus to avert our gaze from them acknowledges the truth that we all began as such embryos, honors the hopes of those who first produced them, or is honest about the possibilities we withhold from them. We could use them in scientific research that would destroy them in the process. But doing that means using them a second time for our own purposes, an unsavory idea that I will take up briefly below. We could thaw them and allow them to die, preferably with their dying surrounded by a religious ritual. That, in fact, is my own preferred solution to a problem with no good solution. Or, finally, we could make them available for "adoption" by women who want to gestate and rear them as their own children.

Although some Christians have been in the forefront of those encouraging embryo adoption, not all Christians approve it. In 2008 the Roman Catholic Church's Congregation for the Doctrine of the Faith (CDF) released an instruction titled *Dignitas Personae*. It was presented as an "update" of an earlier (1987) instruction, *Donum Vitae* (mentioned in chapter 4).[2] After a lengthy discussion of the fundamental human goods at stake and the most recent approaches to assisted reproduction, the instruction addresses directly the existence of frozen embryos, concluding that "the thousands of abandoned embryos represent a *situation of injustice that in fact cannot be resolved.*"[3] That is, none of the possible uses of frozen embryos was deemed ethically acceptable.

This is not as strange or unhelpful a conclusion as it might at first seem. For what it essentially says is that we should stop doing what we have been doing—stop producing surplus embryos that are not implanted and gestated, stop continuing to freeze yet more embryos. If this conclusion does not tell us what to do with the frozen embryos already produced, it does tell us that we should have thought more carefully before plunging ahead with new reproductive technologies, and it does tell us that, seeing where our thoughtlessness has led, we should stop compounding the problem.

But, of course, the already existing frozen embryos will not just disappear. Why not approve adopting them? Would that not, in fact, be in keeping with the Roman Catholic Church's high estimate of embryonic life? (And, to be sure, there are Roman Catholics who argue in favor of embryo adoption.) Although approval might seem to follow from the church's belief that embryos are human beings from the start, *Dignitas Personae* holds that "prenatal adoption" of frozen embryos, like the use of them as a treatment for infertility, "is not ethically acceptable" (19). I will gradually make my way toward a discussion of this view— why one might hold it, and why one might not. But perhaps the best way to develop some sympathy for defenders of embryo adoption is to consider the argumentative lengths to which its critics are prepared to go.

For example, Fr. Tadeusz Pacholczyk, trained not only as a priest but also as a neuroscientist, serves on the staff of the National Catholic Bioethics Center. His position, carefully articulated and argued, is that "an intentional and freely chosen action of embryo adoption, even by a married couple, represents an intrinsically disordered, or inherently evil kind of action, that is to say, an action that cannot ever be rendered morally licit, even by the extenuating circumstances that the embryo finds himself or herself in when cryopreserved and abandoned by his or her own parents."[4] His reasons for taking this view would be shared by at least some others and are in large part the sorts of reasons that led *Dignitas Personae* to reject in vitro fertilization and surrogate motherhood more generally—reasons I will eventually consider.

For the moment, however, I want to note something in Pacholczyk's view that strikes me as astonishing—so astonishing, in fact, as to raise doubts about the persuasiveness of his understanding of human procreation. Addressing the problem of what to do with already existing frozen embryos that are no longer wanted by those who produced them, Pacholczyk essentially agrees with *Dignitas Personae* that there really is no just way to resolve the problem. The best we can do, in his view, is keep them frozen indefinitely, knowing that they may eventually become less viable, degrading in a way somewhat akin to the process of aging and dying.

Given the options as he understands them, that is certainly a reasonable approach. But then, still reaching for a solution, he tries one thought experiment too many. Sometime in the future we might, he speculates, be capable of ectogenesis. That is, we might develop an incubator that would make it possible to thaw the embryos and "gestate" them outside the womb "in an environment completely removed from any maternal influence."[5] Indeed, he offers this speculative possibility as an additional reason for sustaining the surplus embryos indefinitely in their frozen state. At least to me, however, it is astonishing that he should, on the one hand, hold that embryo adoption is intrinsically disordered while, on the other hand, think it acceptable to gestate human beings by means of technology that lacks any relation of child to mother. The dehumanization depicted in Huxley's *Brave New World* is evidently morally preferable to embryo adoption.[6]

This suggests to me that Pacholczyk has not fully appreciated the meaning of procreation, even though its nature plays a central role in his rejection of assisted reproduction and embryo adoption. What a mother provides for her family is "place." Not just a sense of place, but place in a stronger, bodily sense. She is the place from which the child springs and the place that binds the family together. Every child needs a place of belonging, and the mother provides it. What would it mean for our humanity to be "gestated" by a machine, to have no mother who was the place where we belonged, the place that located and identified us? Perhaps embryo adoption provides such a place. That, at least, is a possibility we should think through. It could not possibly be less humane than the "solution" Pacholczyk is prepared to endorse.

Moral Objections

This does not mean that there are no serious objections, worth taking seriously, to embryo adoption. For the most part, these have been put forward by Roman Catholic moralists. Their reasons for concern are primarily three, one involving the effects of embryo adoption on our understanding of the marital relation between husband and wife; another, its effects on the human dignity of the child produced; and yet another, the suggestion that embryo adoption is a form of surrogacy. We can enter this discussion by way of positions put forth in *Dignitas Personae*, positions that raise objections to producing children by means of new reproductive technologies. We have already considered some similar issues in the previous chapter's discussion of assisted reproduction. Here the problem is trying to decide whether roughly the same moral concerns need apply to embryo adoption.

One of the goods of marriage affirmed in *Dignitas Personae* is the "reciprocal respect" of spouses "to become a father or mother only together with the other spouse" (12). This teaching is not intended to prohibit adoption; indeed, the document also affirms that "adoption should be encouraged, promoted, and facilitated" (13).[7] The concern here is simply that, if donated gametes are used to produce a child for the couple, the unity of their marriage (as expressed in procreation) has been broken by the personal presence of a third party (the gamete donor). An asymmetry in their relation to the child has been created, keeping them from becoming "father or mother only together with the other spouse." We might, of course, deny that providing sperm or ovum constitutes personal presence, but, as I noted in the previous chapter, many people do not seem to find that denial persuasive.

Suppose we grant that use of donated gametes does wrong the marriage bond by creating such an asymmetry and that, therefore, we should not produce children by such means. Would the same objection apply to embryo adoption? It seems a stretch to argue that it would. If a married couple decides to use in vitro fertilization to enable the wife to gestate a frozen embryo, it seems right to say that the husband is "a fellow agent in the project of embryo adoption."[8] Together the spouses produce a child whom they intend to raise as a member of their family, and it is hard to deny that they have "become a father or mother only together with the other spouse." Unlike a couple that uses donated sperm or ova for assisted reproduction, this couple has not engaged in a reproductive act. Rather, they have decided that together they will nurture and care for an already existing human being.[9] I cannot see, to use the standard Roman Catholic language, that they have separated the unitive and procreative dimensions of their marriage.

There is, however, a second, equally important consideration. *Dignitas Personae*, citing *Donum Vitae*, affirms that "'procreation of a human person [should] be brought about as the fruit of the conjugal act specific to the love between spouses'" (12).[10] The reason for this is perhaps a bit underdeveloped in *Dignitas Personae*, which simply asserts that this requirement grows out of "the specifically human values of sexuality" (12). But, clearly, the concern is for the human dignity of the child produced. The point is that a child produced by means of reproductive technology is less a blessing bestowed upon the sexual love husband and wife share than an object produced to satisfy their desires. As such—as one who is "made" rather than "begotten"—the child is no longer clearly equal in dignity with his or her parents. If we affirm the child's equal dignity, we do so only as an act of will or choice, not as the recognition of a birthright.

Suppose we grant that this should rightly give us reason for moral concern about assisted reproduction. Should it also give us reason to draw back from embryo adoption? Once again, the force of the argument seems hard to discern. To be sure, some people did "make" this embryonic life, but the adopting parents did not. What they have done is take into their family for nurture and care an already existing human being. Like all adoptive parents, they become parents without procreating.

There is a remaining concern about embryo adoption, mentioned but not developed in *Dignitas Personae*—namely, that one might regard the adopting mother as a surrogate, who uses her body simply to incubate a child. In stating this objection *Dignitas Personae* (19) is content to refer back to the more developed argument in *Donum Vitae* II, A, 1–3. And *Donum Vitae* rejects surrogacy for the two reasons discussed above—namely, that it separates love-giving from life-giving within the bond of marriage, and that it fails to respect fully the dignity of the child. Underlying these reasons for concern is the sense that in surrogacy a woman's body becomes less the place of her personal presence than a device used to accomplish a desired end (even if, admittedly, a worthy end).

Does this concern, a serious one, give reason to disapprove embryo adoption? I think not—at least, not if we attend carefully to what *Donum Vitae* actually says. For, as a footnote to its text makes clear, *Donum Vitae* understands surrogacy necessarily to involve an intention to surrender the baby after birth to whoever commissioned the reproductive project in which the surrogate has participated.[11] In one form of surrogacy (usually called traditional, or genetic) a woman who agrees to serve as surrogate is artificially inseminated by donor sperm, completes the pregnancy, and then surrenders the child (presumably to the sperm donor). In another form, a surrogate gestates an embryo produced in vitro with donated gametes and has no genetic relation to the child she carries. And again, she surrenders the child after birth to those who commissioned and recruited her for this reproductive project. In either case, however, central to *Donum Vitae*'s understanding of surrogacy is that the woman who becomes pregnant intends from the outset to surrender the baby after it has been born.

Our question now becomes: Is embryo adoption a form of surrogacy (as *Donum Vitae* characterizes it)? Evidently not, at least if the woman and her husband intend to rear this child as their own. For then their commitment to the child is the kind of permanent commitment that parents make. This makes clear, in fact, why we would be mistaken to think of embryo adoption as "rescue," or attempt to justify it in those terms. Presumably a healthy woman of the appropriate age could be a surrogate who "rescues" (and then surrenders) a frozen embryo roughly once a year. That would be something quite different from what it means to be a child's mother, and in that case the woman would indeed be using her body simply as a kind of incubator. We can grant the nobility of her motives, as we could for someone endorsing ectogenesis to "rescue" frozen embryos, but good motives are not the only moral consideration. John Berkman seems right when he says that a woman "rescuing" a frozen embryo by gestating and then surrendering it would be "acting contrary to a fundamental good of parenthood, namely permanence."[12]

One might suggest, as E. Christian Brugger has, that motherhood (or, for that matter, fatherhood) need not involve a permanent commitment. Imagine someone becoming an emergency adoptive mother for a child already born, intending to perform this role only temporarily. Brugger argues that this would not fall short in any way of genuine parenthood.[13] But his is far too purely conceptual a notion of what it means to be a father or mother. To think of it as a temporary role means that one must guard against making too strong an emotional commitment to the child; for if that commitment becomes too deep, giving up the child will scar both parents and child. (That, in fact, is one reason why being a foster parent is such an emotionally delicate task.) But to guard against too deep a commitment because one knows the commitment to be temporary is incompatible with the parental role.

Taken together, then, these three angles of vision, carefully developed especially in Roman Catholic moral theology, do not offer good reasons for disapproving embryo adoption. These concerns—for the inseparability of love-giving and life-giving within marriage, for children who are not products but who share with us an equal human dignity, and for a woman's body as the place of her personal presence and not simply an incubator available for accomplishing good purposes—raise serious moral concerns about many forms of assisted reproduction. But they do not seem to apply in the same way to embryo adoption carried out by a husband and wife who are committed to rearing any child born to them.

Shall we then encourage married couples to press forward with the project of embryo adoption, thereby providing a familial place of belonging for embryos who, because of our culture's heedlessness, have been left abandoned in a kind of frozen limbo? We are not, I think, ready to conclude that. Several other ways of dealing with the thousands of cryopreserved embryos need to be considered. First among these, at least in the minds of some whose focus is especially on scientific progress, is the possibility that these embryos might be a source of valuable material for research.

Research Using Spare Embryos

Research using stem cells derived from human embryos has been a controversial topic within public policy arguments for most of the last twenty years for the simple reason that disaggregating an embryo in order to obtain its stem cells means the death of the embryo. Using frozen embryos that were once intended for use in someone's assisted reproduction project but are no longer needed or wanted for that purpose is an important subset of that topic. A policy that permits the use and destruction of such "spare" embryos in research while prohibiting the creation of embryos intended from the outset as research subjects has been seen by many as a compromise that could at least in part satisfy the concerns of opposing sides in the dispute.

Indeed, after eight years in which the administration of George W. Bush declined to fund any research on stem cells derived from newly destroyed human embryos, in 2009 the National Institutes of Health under the Obama administration permitted and encouraged such funding, but only if the stem cells had been derived from embryos "that were created using in vitro fertilization for reproductive purposes and were no longer needed for that purpose."[14] Only, in short, from so-called spare embryos, but not from embryos created simply to be used (and in the process destroyed) in research.

What makes this seem like an attractive compromise to some people? The reason is quite simple and, at first sight, might seem persuasive. Because spare embryos are destined to be discarded in any case—because, that is, those with legal authority over these frozen embryos have decided not to use them for reproductive purposes and, eventually, to discard them—they have no future life prospects. They are destined to die, and the only question is how. Why not, one might wonder, gain some useful knowledge from their dying? This may seem more attractive than simply approving embryo research without limits.

Offered as a compromise, such an approach has what might be called a distinguished pedigree. Something like it was specifically endorsed by the National Bioethics Advisory Commission in its 1999 report *Ethical Issues in Human Stem Cell Research*.[15] The Commission recommended that research on stem cells derived from embryos remaining after infertility treatments should be eligible for federal funding but that, at least for a time, such funding not be available for research on stem cells derived from embryos that had been produced solely for research purposes. Nevertheless, that precedent notwithstanding, we should not too quickly endorse such research. For, as it happens, the historical pedigree of this sort of reasoning is actually rather mixed and troubling. Two examples will make the point.

Perhaps the most well-known instance of research in the United States that is now generally agreed to have been wrong is the Tuskegee syphilis experiment. For approximately forty years officials of the U.S. Public Health Service studied the course of untreated syphilis by using impoverished and uneducated black men in Macon County, Alabama, as research subjects. The men were left untreated even after penicillin was known to be effective in the treatment of patients with syphilis. Shocking as this may now seem, the researchers did not lack a rationale to support their work. After all, the poverty, illiteracy, and race of these men meant that, even if the research had not been undertaken, they almost surely would not have received treatment. The circumstances of their lives destined them to suffer from and perhaps die of complications resulting from syphilis.

Public Health officials were not in a position to change those circumstances. Carrying out their research would neither diminish the life prospects of these men nor impose upon them any additional risk of harm. Why not, therefore, at least gain from their plight knowledge that might benefit future sufferers? In *Bad Blood: The Tuskegee Syphilis Experiment*, James H. Jones describes that rationale: "The fate of syphilitic blacks in Macon County was sealed (at least for the immediate future) regardless of whether an experiment went forward. Increasing the store of knowledge seemed the only way to profit from the suffering there."[16] Nothing is lost. Useful medical knowledge may be gained. Why not proceed?

A second example of this sort of reasoning is, if anything, more thought-provoking still. When prisoners arrived at a concentration camp such as Auschwitz, "selections" were made that determined the life prospects of those prisoners. These selections meant that some of the prisoners would certainly die; they had no future life prospects. Discussing the way in which doctors at Auschwitz, who needed surgical experience, must have reasoned, Robert Jay Lifton writes: "In the absence of ethical restraint, one could arrange exactly the kind of surgical experience one sought, on exactly the appropriate kinds of 'cases' at exactly the time one wanted. If one felt Hippocratic twinges of conscience, one could usually reassure oneself that, since all of these people were condemned to death in any case, one was not really harming them."[17]

That reasoning is striking, and we have met it before. By virtue of decisions others had made, these victims had no life prospects. Hence, they could not really be harmed if subjected to experiments that would never have been carried out on people not destined to die. Why not, then, gain useful medical knowledge and thereby salvage some good from tragic circumstances? It was not hard for the doctors about whom Lifton writes, who supposed themselves to be advancing the mission of medicine, to adopt such a line of reasoning.

I do not say that those who support research on spare embryos should be equated with the Tuskegee researchers or the Nazi doctors. I simply offer these examples as an invitation to wonder whether the supposed compromise on frozen embryos—research on "spares" but no others—is really so appealing. There are, I believe, reasons to question the appeal of this approach.

Frozen, "spare" embryos have already been used once in the service of someone else's reproductive project, used to satisfy the desires of others. And being used once is enough. If they are no longer needed or wanted for reproductive purposes, we should not suppose that they are still available for our use, still a handy resource for other purposes entirely unrelated to their well-being or their natural end. The fact that our own choices have destined them to die should not make them available for our continued use.

What follows, we might ask, from the fact that they are destined to die? Not that we should feel free to use them in our research projects, but, rather, that, as Hans Jonas once argued with respect to the terminally ill, we should spare them "the gratu-itousness of service to an unrelated cause."[18] Given that certain choices have been made, these spare embryos are destined to die, but our relation to their dying is not a matter for moral indifference. It is one thing for us to accept the fact that we have no way readily available to offer them continued life. It is quite another for us to welcome their death as an advantageous opportunity to use them once again for purposes entirely unrelated to their own well-being. First we determine that they must die. Then we say that, since they're destined to die anyway, we might as well gain some good from that tragedy. As a moral argument that is hard to recommend.

Is Adoption the Solution?

If we resist the lure of using frozen embryos as research subjects, what alternatives remain? Evidently just two. We can thaw the embryos, allowing them to die, or we can encourage willing couples to implant and gestate them in the hope of giving birth to children for whom they will be adoptive parents.

The second alternative, embryo adoption, may be pursued for different reasons. For some Christian people, in particular, it is a way of being on the side of life, offering themselves as adoptive parents for a child who would otherwise never be able to develop and mature.[19] No doubt such adoptive parents are often moved by more than one motive, desiring both to be parents and to give the possibility of continued life to an abandoned embryo. For others it may be chiefly a new avenue for dealing with infertility. Rather than pursuing in vitro fertilization, they may choose to implant and gestate an already existing (frozen) embryo.[20] But in either case, embryos that might have remained frozen indefinitely or could have been thawed and permitted to die will have parents who, we could say, adopt them even before parturition.

If we think, as I do, that these embryos are human beings who ought not to be kept indefinitely in a frozen limbo, should we then encourage their adoption (whatever the particular motives of those who adopt)? My own view, as I indicated at the beginning of this chapter, is that we should not encourage embryo adoption. This is not because I think the arguments against it, made chiefly by Roman Catholic moralists, are persuasive. Rather, the reason is a much simpler one. As I noted in chapter three, there are estimated to be almost 18 million orphans worldwide. These are children already born, who have lost both parents. It does not even include children whose parents are living but who have been abusive or neglectful, from whose custody the children have been taken. If we are looking for children in need of adoption, children likely to suffer still more harm if they have no familial place of belonging, they are all around us. My intuition, of which I will try to make a little sense in what follows, is that these children have the greater claim on us for adoption.

It might seem—and perhaps does seem to some—that taking such a position inevitably undermines the claim that embryos are human beings with claims upon us equal to the claims of those who are already born. After all, children already born have capabilities and characteristics that are far more developed than those of embryos, who have little more than the capacity for further development. If we systematically favor the claims of those already born for adoption, passing by available cryopreserved embryos, are we not in effect saying that those whose capacities are more developed have greater worth?

Put in specifically Christian and biblical language, we might say that the embryos frozen in limbo are "the least" of Jesus's brothers and sisters, whom he teaches his followers to care for and serve.[21] What we do for the weak and vulnerable we do, he says, for him. There are, nonetheless, good reasons to hold that our limited energy and resources for adoption should be directed toward children already born.

In a very different context far removed from these particular issues, Reinhold Niebuhr distinguished the equality of sin from the inequality of guilt, while noting that Christians affirm and emphasize both. "Guilt is distinguished from sin in that it represents the objective and historical consequences of sin, for which the sinner must be held responsible."[22] Niebuhr's point was that when we hold people responsible for "the objective and historical" harms their actions have caused, treating them in a way we do not treat those whose actions have not similarly harmed others, we do not signify that some are more sinful than others. On the contrary, before God all human beings are equally sinners, even though they are not equally guilty of harming others. If, pointing to the truth that all of us are equally sinners, we fail to hold the guilty responsible for the harmful consequences of their actions, we are not protecting those who have suffered harm. And, at the same time, if we suppose that unequal guilt means that some are more sinful than others, we lose the truth that all of us are equidistant from the transcendent God. That God-relation makes us equals, though without destroying the inequalities that are apparent in human history.

We should, I think, make a somewhat analogous move in thinking about who has the greater claim upon us for adoption. Children already born need a mother and a father; they need a familial place of belonging. Lacking this they are very likely to be harmed in serious and predictable ways. They may be developmentally delayed in ways that can never be overcome, whatever educational opportunities they receive. Perhaps more important, lacking the assurance that they belong, lacking a bond with their parents from an early age, they may be hard to handle and difficult to control. Too many of them may never feel at home in the world, and too many of them may end in institutions of one sort or another. We will have failed them in ways that pile one harm upon another.

To say, then, that their need for adoption takes priority over that of frozen embryos is not to make any judgment about greater or lesser human worth, greater or lesser personal dignity. It is simply to acknowledge the significant historical harms these children will suffer if they are not adopted. Cryopreserved embryos, by contrast, do not experience new harms if left in their current state. To be sure, we have wronged them by using assisted reproduction technologies in ways that have left so many nascent human lives in this tenuous state, and we will be morally responsible if we continue such practices. But we can hold that these embryos and children already born are of equal human worth—each of them one of us—without thinking that we must therefore treat them precisely the same. Equal status does not require identical treatment, as every parent with more than one child knows well.

If our resources for adoption were limitless, the argument might have a different look. But they are not. And because they are not, the distinction between positive and negative duties makes a difference here. Negative duties obligate us not to do wrong to others—to any other—in a variety of ways. They apply without fail to everyone with whom we come into contact. Positive duties obligate us to bring aid to others, when we can and to the degree that we can, but they do not specify what our actions should be. For there are countless people to whom we might bring aid, and we have to decide when and where our capacities for helping can make the most difference and which possible recipients of our aid have the greatest claim upon us. There is no cookbook recipe for answering that question, but it is plausible to suggest that children with whom we are already interacting in a variety of ways should be the primary focus of our attention and action.

Of course, if my argument is persuasive, we are left with the question of what to do with frozen embryos, which are no longer needed or wanted for reproductive purposes by those who produced them, but which will not be adopted. We could, I suppose, simply leave them frozen indefinitely, recognizing that over time their condition might degrade to the point where they could not be thawed and gestated successfully, even if one wished to do so. But that approach—polite avoidance—hardly seems to recognize and value the dignity they share with us. If they are going to die, we should honor and accompany them in their dying.

We do that best if we thaw them, recognizing of course that they cannot survive for long in an environment that is not a mother's womb. In doing this we are letting them die—victims, we might say, of our culture's rush to assisted reproduction. But this approach will not be satisfactory if it simply means removing the embryos from frozen storage and disposing of them without further thought. What Christians, at least, should want is a brief religious ritual to accompany their dying, a liturgy in which we commend these weakest of human beings to God, though perhaps also a liturgy in which with the psalmists we ask God how long his providence will permit this to continue.

I realize, of course, that this recommendation may be thought whimsical. Someone might ask, as Austin Farrer once put it in a rather different context, how we can "relate to the mercy of God beings who never enjoy a glimmer of reason."[23] Farrer himself was willing at least to consider (without being entirely persuaded by) the possibility that "every human birth, however imperfect, is the germ of a personality" to which God can give "an eternal future."[24] Probably, though, we simply have to acknowledge that here we meet a mystery beyond our ability to fathom. What we should not do, however, is allow ourselves to be so taken by the mystery that we lose sight of the many children, already born, who desperately need from us a place of familial belonging.

We demonstrate our humanity by accompanying frozen embryos to their death and committing them liturgically to God's care. We demonstrate that same humanity by not allowing our gaze to be diverted from the many children likely to suffer irreparable harm if they are not adopted.

Conclusion

"'I thought Marilla Cuthbert was an old fool when I heard she'd adopted a girl out of an orphan asylum,' she said to herself, 'but I guess she didn't make much of a mistake after all. If I'd a child like Anne in the house all the time I'd be a better and happier woman.'"[1] Those are the private thoughts of Miss Josephine Berry in what may be the most engaging novel ever written about an adopted child, L. M. Montgomery's *Anne of Green Gables*, first published in 1908 and set on Prince Edward Island. Although coming half a century or so after the heyday of the Romantic movement, the story clearly finds in nature something of enormous significance.

Yet, at the same time, it is a story not about a child and her "natural" parents but about adoption, about how the history that grows up between Anne Shirley and Marilla and Matthew Cuthbert shapes a home that gives all three of them a place of belonging. In this way the story very nicely puts flesh on the words of Pope John Paul II, which I cited earlier in chapter 3: "To adopt a child is a great *work of love*. When it is done, much is given, but much is also received. It is a true exchange of gifts."[2] To trace this theme briefly through *Anne of Green Gables* gives us a way to uncover once again the truth at the heart of adoption.

At the outset Matthew and Marilla Cuthbert (older, unmarried siblings) have in mind a rather different sort of exchange of gifts. They want to adopt a ten- or eleven-year-old boy—old enough to begin to help with chores around the farm, and increasingly able to do so as, over the years, Matthew needs more help. But they do truly intend the relationship to be an exchange. "We mean to give him a good home and schooling," Marilla says to her neighbor, Mrs. Lynde (6). Through a mix-up that only later they come to regard as providential, however, they are sent an eleven-year-old girl, Anne (with an *e*, as she is always careful to insist). Her parents had been teachers, but both had died just three months after her birth. She lived for a time with a woman whose husband was often drunk and who took her in so that Anne could help care for her four younger children. After that she lived with another woman who needed help caring for her eight children. When the second woman died, Anne ended up at the orphanage in Nova Scotia, from where Marilla and Matthew take her.

Matthew, an inordinately shy man who says as little as possible, goes to meet her at the train station. He cannot bring himself to tell her that there has been a mistake, and, since he can hardly leave her to spend the night alone at the train station, he takes her back to Green Gables with him. Anne, who talks nonstop on the ride, says to him at one point: "Oh, it seems so wonderful that I'm going to live with you and belong to you. I've never belonged to anybody—not really" (12).

As those who have read the story know, Anne is a wonderfully engaging character, whom it is hard to resist. By the time they have made the ride to Green Gables, Matthew has pretty much fallen in love with her and wants to keep her, the mix-up notwithstanding. Marilla, though, is a cautious, more realistic soul. From her perspective a mistake has been made. It should be rectified as quickly as possible—and Anne returned. "What good would she be to us?" Marilla asks, reasonably enough. " 'We might be some good to her,' said Matthew suddenly and unexpectedly" (27). The language of mutual exchange seems to come naturally to him. And, though it perhaps is less natural for Marilla, she cannot find it in her heart to send this young girl who so desperately longs for a home back to the orphanage.

Anne talks constantly, she is scatter-brained, and she loses herself frequently in the beauties of nature and the wonders her powerful imagination conjures up. As a result, she frequently finds herself in embarrassing situations, makes mistakes, and loses track of time. Once Marilla sends Anne into another room to get something. She waits and waits for Anne to return. Finally, after ten minutes or so, she goes in search of her and finds Anne standing motionless, looking at a picture of Jesus blessing little children. As Anne explains to Marilla,

> I was just imagining I was one of them—that I was the little girl in the blue dress, standing off by herself in the corner as if she didn't belong to anybody, like me. She looks lonely and sad, don't you think? I guess she hadn't any father or mother of her own. But she wanted to be blessed too, so she just crept shyly up on the outside of the crowd, hoping nobody would notice her—except Him. I'm sure I know just how she felt. Her heart must have beat and her hands must have got cold, like mine did when I asked you if I could stay. She was afraid He mightn't notice her. But it's likely He did, don't you think? I've been trying to imagine it all out—her edging a little nearer all the time until she was quite close to Him; and then He would look at her and pat His hand on her hair and oh, such a thrill of joy as would run over her! (55)

And even unimaginative Marilla can sense how important it is for this young girl to find a place of belonging.

Gradually their shared life begins to make of them a true family. Walking home one evening with Marilla, Anne suddenly slips her hand into Marilla's and says, "It's lovely to be going home and know it's home" (74). Perhaps to her own surprise, Marilla also begins to feel that she genuinely wants and needs Anne's presence. When Anne has been gone for just a few days with her friend Diana Berry, Marilla is very glad to have her return. "I'm glad you've got back, I must say. It's been fearful lonesome here without you, and I never put in four longer days," she says to Anne (230).

By the time Anne is fifteen, she is clearly at home with Marilla and Matthew. Having completed her basic schooling, Anne plans to go to the teachers' college located in Charlottetown, which means that she will have to be away from home during the academic year. Much as they hate to see her go, Matthew and Marilla understand that this too is part of what it means to provide a home for a child. And they do not forget what she has given them. "She's been a blessing to us," Matthew thinks to himself, "and there never was a luckier mistake than what Mrs. Spencer made—if it is *was* luck. I don't believe it was any such thing. It was Providence, because the Almighty saw we needed her" (269). At the teachers' academy Anne's work is so good that she is awarded a prize that will enable her to continue her education and earn a B. A. But when Matthew dies suddenly, Marilla is left alone, burdened with a doctor's diagnosis that she is in danger of losing her eyesight. Anne relinquishes the prize, takes a teaching position, and remains at Green Gables with Marilla. The mutual exchange has come full circle.

Time and history have made of them a family—not a fictive one, but a real one. Hence, even Marilla, reluctant as she is to express emotion, says to Anne shortly after Matthew's death: "I want to tell you now when I can. It's never been easy for me to say things out of my heart, but at times like this it's easier. I love you as dear as if you were my own flesh and blood and you've been my joy and comfort ever since you came to Green Gables" (288).

This brings us back to where we began, puzzling over the relation between nature and history. Some puzzles we may not be able to resolve entirely, but for Christians one thing should be clear. Marilla cannot be mistaken to believe that the familial history she shares with Anne has bound them together every bit as much as if they were related by blood. Not flesh and blood but *huiothesia* will inherit the kingdom. Because we know that, we should be especially open to the truth Marilla perceives and, finally, speaks. And therefore, without in any way failing to appreciate the beauty and importance of the created familial bonds into which God places us, we can see in them intimations of a still greater family formed not by nature but by grace: the grace of adoption.

Notes

Introduction

1. Luke 1:60–63. Biblical quotations, unless otherwise indicated, are from the Revised Standard Version.
2. Luke 3:8.
3. Romans 11:17–18.

CHAPTER 1. Nature and History

1. Marianne Novy, *Reading Adoption: Family and Difference in Fiction and Drama* (Ann Arbor: University of Michigan Press, 2005), 39.
2. Novy, *Reading Adoption*, 48.
3. Novy, *Reading Adoption*, 39.
4. George Eliot, *Silas Marner: The Weaver of Raveloe* (London: Heritage Press, n.d.), 165. References will be given by page number in parentheses within the body of the text.
5. Novy, *Reading Adoption*, 154.
6. Novy, *Reading Adoption*, 156.
7. George Eliot, *Daniel Deronda*, vols. 1 and 2 (New York: Thomas Nelson and Sons, 1920), 1:574–75. Future references will be given by volume and page number in parentheses within the body of the text.
8. Novy, *Reading Adoption*, 148.

9. Russell D. Moore, *Adopted for Life: The Priority of Adoption for Christian Families and Churches* (Wheaton, IL: Crossway Books, 2009). References will be given by page number in parentheses within the body of the text.

10. Recently (in 2015) Moore brought out an updated and expanded version of his book. He now grants that the claims of nature may be a little stronger than he at first acknowledged. Thus, he writes of his adopted sons: "They are who they were, but nurtured and directed. They are Moores and have become like the rest of the family, and the rest of the family has become more like them. In their lives I see a mirror of what the gospel does. In adopting us and in regenerating us, God does not obliterate our personalities and distinctiveness." This goes a long way toward providing the kind of nuance that is needed and that his original edition did not fully have. See Russell Moore, *Adopted for Life*, updated and expanded ed. (Wheaton, IL: Crossway Books, 2015), 224.

11. In fact, something like this is also Paul's view about Israel; they too are God's people not simply by birth but by adoption. Thus, in Romans 9:4 he says of the Israelites that (in the RSV translation) "to them belong[s] the sonship." The word translated here as "sonship" is *huiothesia*, which means, literally, "the act of placing [someone] as a son" or "the act of giving [someone] the place of a son." Hence, the King James translation speaks of Israelites as those "to whom pertaineth the adoption." The New English Bible reads, "They were made God's sons." This seems to mean that Israel was chosen by God out of all the nations. Even Israelites have no natural claim on a relation to God.

12. Paul Robert Sauer, "Adoption after Altruism," *Lutheran Forum* 42 (Winter 2008): 11–13. References will be given by page number in parentheses within the body of the text.

13. In the updated edition of *Adopted for Life* Russell Moore also underscores this point more strongly than he did in the first edition: "We would have no adoption, no foster care, no orphan ministry in an unfallen world" (159).

14. David Pearl and Werner Menski, *Muslim Family Law*, 3rd ed. (London: Sweet & Maxwell, 1998), 408.

15. Ingrid Mattson, "Adoption and Fostering," *Encyclopedia of Women & Islamic Cultures* (Boston: Brill, 2005), 2:1.

16. Mattson, "Adoption and Fostering," 1.

17. Mattson, "Adoption and Fostering," 1.

18. Muslim Women's Shura Council, *Adoption and the Care of Orphan Children: Islam and the Best Interests of the Child* (2011), 5, http://www.wisemuslimwomen.org/images/activism/Adoption_(August_2011)_Final.pdf. At the beginning of this position paper, the Shura Council describes itself as "a global and inclusive council of Muslim women scholars, activists, and specialists. The Shura Council connects Islamic principles to society's most pressing issues and develops holistic strategies for positive social change."

19. Muslim Women's Shura Council, "Adoption and the Care of Orphan Children," 17.

20. Michael Gold, "Adoption: A New Problem for Jewish Law," *Judaism* 36 (Fall 1987): 444. Thus, remembering the first puzzle above, we can observe that Daniel Deronda was a Jew, whether he realized it or not.

21. See, for example, "Gestational Surrogacy Raises Question of 'Who Is a Jew,'" *Haaretz*, September 30, 2014, http://www.haaretz.com/.

22. More information about this debate can be found on the website of the Institute for Dayanim at http://www.dinonline.org/. See also the Wikipedia article "Yichud," http://en.wikipedia.org.

23. Michael J. Broyde, "Adoption, Personal Status, and Jewish Law," in *The Morality of Adoption*, ed. Timothy P. Jackson (Grand Rapids: Eerdmans, 2005), 147.

24. Gold, "Adoption," 443.

25. Shelley Kapnek Rosenberg, *Adoption and the Jewish Family: Contemporary Perspectives* (Philadelphia and Jerusalem: Jewish Publication Society, 1998), 193.

26. Noah Millman, "True Fictions of Fatherhood," *First Things*, February 2004, 16.

27. Joseph B. Soloveitchik, "Parenthood: Natural and Redeemed," in *Family Redeemed: Essays on Family Relationships*, ed. David Shatz and Joel B. Wolowelsky (New York: Toras Horav Foundation, 2000), 105–25. References will be given by page number within the body of the text. My thanks to Rabbi Mark Gottlieb for directing my attention to this essay.

28. John Paul II, "Address of the Holy Father John Paul II to the Meeting of the Adoptive Families Organized by the Missionaries of Charity," September 5, 2000, http://www.vatican.va/.

29. P. D. Eastman, *Are You My Mother?* (New York: Random House, 1960).

30. Keiko Kasza, *A Mother for Choco* (New York: Puffin Books, 1992).

31. Russ Richter, "Reflections on Adoption and Religion," in *The Spirit of Adoption: Writers on Religion, Adoption, Faith, and More*, ed. Melanie Springer Mock, Martha Kalnin Diede, and Jeremiah Webster (Eugene, OR: Cascade Books, 2014), 135–46.

32. Richter, "Reflections," 135.

33. John Berkman, "Virtuous Parenting and Orphaned Embryos," in *Human Embryo Adoption: Biotechnology, Marriage, and the Right to Life*, ed. Edward Furton and Thomas Berg (Philadelphia: National Catholic Bioethics Center Press, 2006), 23.

CHAPTER 2. Adoptees One and All

1. Karl Barth, *Church Dogmatics*, III/4 (Edinburgh: T. & T. Clark, 1961), 243.

2. Barth, *Church Dogmatics*, III/4, 277.

3. Because translations of the New Testament do not consistently translate *huiothesia* in any single way, and because my interest here is in thinking through the language of adoption, I will not follow any single translation but will draw on several in order to trace this theme. Moreover, contemporary readers should not imagine that "adoption as sons" is the language of an earlier, now politically incorrect, era. After all, the King James Version translates *huiothesia* in Ephesians 1:5 as "adoption of children." But the defect of a translation that lacks the language of "sonship" is that it does not highlight the way in which adoption into Christ, the Son of the Father, brings believers into a relationship of sonship with his Father. Thus, Geordie Ziegler comments: "Because in the first century only men could hold property, to be adopted was to be 'placed as a son' within a family system. In first-century culture, the adoption preserved the estate of the deceased. While the slave could not inherit the owner's property, the son would. 'Sonship' is not sexist language; it is about receiving a relationship that comes entirely as gift." "Trinitarian Adoption and Identity Formation," in Mock, Diede, and Webster, *Spirit of Adoption*, 4.

4. Trevor J. Burke, *Adopted into God's Family: Exploring a Pauline Metaphor* (Downers Grove, IL: InterVarsity Press, 2006), 61.

5. Francis Lyall, "Roman Law in the Writings of Paul— Adoption," *Journal of Biblical Literature* 88 (December 1969): 464.

6. Lyall, "Roman Law," 466. Probably the most famous example of such adoption in Roman history would be the adoption of Octavian, as a young man, to be the son of Julius Caesar. Octavian became heir to the empire and is known to us as Caesar Augustus.

7. Nor was it a legal fiction in Roman law, as Trevor Burke notes when recounting the adoption of Nero as son and successor of Emperor Claudius. It happened that Claudius already had a daughter, Octavia. Though she had no biological (blood) relation to Nero, his adoption made them legally brother and sister. When later they wished to marry, special legislation was needed to make this possible. That it was needed shows that after the adoption Nero "was legally in every way considered the same as a natural born son." See Burke, *Adopted into God's Family*, 62.

8. E. Schweizer, "*huiothesia*," in *Theological Dictionary of the New Testament*, ed. Gerhard Friedrich, trans. Geoffrey W. Bromiley (Grand Rapids: Eerdmans, 1972), 8:399.

9. Luke 3:8.

10. Pheme Perkins, *Abraham's Divided Children: Galatians and the Politics of Faith* (Harrisburg, PA: Trinity Press International, 2001), 80.

11. Translations generally say that every "family" in heaven and on earth takes its name from God the Father. This, however, does not fully capture the linguistic connection made in vv. 14–15: All fatherhood (*patria*) takes its name from the Father (*pater*). Thus, every group of persons united by a common ancestor is, in the end, named for the One God who is Father of all and from whom human parenthood comes.

12. Acts 17:29.

13. Barth, *Church Dogmatics*, II/1, 510.

14. Michael Banner, *The Ethics of Everyday Life* (Oxford: Oxford University Press, 2014), 45–46.

15. Banner, *Ethics of Everyday Life*, 46.

16. This theological context helps to explain why, according to Jack Goody, the influence of Christianity made adoption less prominent in the West for centuries. Cf. Jack Goody, *The Development of the Family and Marriage in Europe* (Cambridge: Cambridge University Press, 1983), 72–73. This was not due to any lack of concern for orphaned children. "Instead of guardianship by kin, the early Church made arrangements to look after its own, who were thus protected from being assigned to non-members of the sect at the death of their parents" (74). Later, godparents filled this role, and "adoption was to some

extent replaced by godparenthood, spiritual kinship was preferred to fictional kinship, and indeed to the wider ties of kinship itself" (75). It may be too unnuanced, however, to say that adoption was simply discouraged in Europe. For example, in *Blood Ties and Fictive Ties: Adoption and Family Life in Early Modern France* (Princeton, NJ: Princeton University Press, 1996), Kristin Elizabeth Gager offers evidence to support the claim that, at least in sixteenth- and seventeenth-century Paris, adoption was practiced by some.

17. Barth himself provides a succinct description of his approach in three places: (1) 549–50 of volume II/2 of the *Church Dogmatics*; (2) 24–26 of volume III/4; and (3) 6–11 of *The Christian Life*, a fragment of the unfinished discussion of the ethics of reconciliation in volume IV.

18. Ted Peters, *For the Love of Children: Genetic Technology and the Future of the Family* (Louisville: Westminster John Knox, 1996), 25. Peters has several formulations of the inheritance myth, and they do not always amount to precisely the same thing. Thus, shortly after the passage cited—in which biological inheritance is simply set over against promised future as two seemingly exclusive possibilities—Peters writes that the inheritance myth is "the misleading assumption that the biological connection between parents and children is definitive of their relationship" (26). But, of course, one can grant that it is not definitive without supposing that its significance is entirely lost when we look to the future God has promised.

19. Peters, *For the Love of Children*, 155.

20. Don S. Browning, "Adoption and the Moral Significance of Kin Altruism," in Jackson, *Morality of Adoption*, 67.

21. Richter, "Reflections," 138.

22. In *Adopted for Life*, a book that has many virtues, Russell Moore describes adoption as "a Great Commission priority," referring to Jesus's command in Matthew 28:18–20 to make disciples of all nations through baptism and teaching. But the idea that we should encourage adoption as a method for evangelism comes perilously close to transforming a work of love into a method for manipulating souls. Better, I think, to see adoption simply as a happy exchange of gifts between needy children and would-be adoptive parents. Cf. Moore, *Adopted for Life*, 181.

23. Melissa Moschella, "The Rights of Children: Biology Matters," *Public Discourse*, February 20, 2014, http://www.thepublicdiscourse .com. Moschella offers a more nuanced view in a later essay, "To Whom Do Children Belong? A Defense of Parental Authority," *Public Dis-*

course, October 6, 2015, http://www.thepublicdiscourse.com: "While the ideal is for the biological, psychological and moral aspects of parenthood to be unified, adoptive parents *are* true parents psychologically and morally, and thus more fully parents than those whose parenthood is *merely* biological."

24. Gabriel Marcel, *Homo Viator* (South Bend, IN: St. Augustine's Press, 2010), 111.

25. Marcel, *Homo Viator*, 117.

26. Augustine, sermons 51 and 40, in *Sermons III (51–94) on the New Testament*, trans. Edmund Hill, O. P. (Brooklyn, NY: New City Press, 1991).

27. Jeremy Cook, "When Adoption, Colorado Ranches, and *Kung Fu Panda* Collide," in Mock, Diede, and Webster, *Spirit of Adoption*, 22.

28. William Werpehowski, "The Vocation of Parenthood: A Response to Stephen Post," *Journal of Religious Ethics* 25, no. 1 (1997): 177.

29. Stephen G. Post, "Adoption Theologically Considered," *Journal of Religious Ethics* 25, no. 1 (1997): 150.

30. Post, "Adoption Theologically Considered," 154–55.

31. Elizabeth Kirk, "Is Adoption Second-Best to a 'Real Family'?," Aleteia, November 24, 2014, http://www.aleteia.org/.

32. Werpehowski, "Vocation of Parenthood," 181.

33. Kirk, "Is Adoption Second-Best?"

34. Banner, *Ethics of Everyday Life*, 80–81.

35. Brent Waters, *The Family in Christian Social and Political Thought* (Oxford: Oxford University Press, 2007), 215.

36. Waters, *Family*, 215.

37. Waters, *Family*, 198.

38. Brent Waters, "Adoption, Parentage, and Procreative Stewardship," in Jackson, *Morality of Adoption*, 41.

39. Emily Yoffe, Dear Prudence: Advice on Manners and Morals, *Slate*, December 18, 2014, http://www.slate.com/articles/life/dear_prudence/2014/12/dear_prudence_my_family_teases_to_show_affection_but_my_boyfriend_doesn.2.html.

40. Maïa de la Baume, "In France, a Baby Switch and a Lesson in Maternal Love," *New York Times*, February 24, 2015, http://www.nytimes.com.

41. Philip Turner, *Ethics and the Church: Ecclesial Foundations for Moral Thought and Practice* (Grand Rapids: Baker Academic, 2015), ix.

42. Turner, *Ethics and the Church*, 67.

43. Turner, *Ethics and the Church*, xi.

44. Turner, *Ethics and the Church*, xi.

45. Turner, *Ethics and the Church*, xx.

CHAPTER 3. Q & A

1. Adam Pertman, *Adoption Nations: How the Adoption Revolution Is Transforming America* (New York: Basic Books, 2000), x.

2. Moore, *Adopted for Life*, 106.

3. Elizabeth Bartholet, *Family Bonds: Adoption and the Politics of Parenting* (Boston: Houghton Mifflin, 1993), xxi.

4. Marcel, *Homo Viator*, 117.

5. John Paul II, "Address of the Holy Father John Paul II to the Meeting of the Adoptive Families Organized by the Missionaries of Charity."

6. P. D. James, *Innocent Blood* (New York: Charles Scribner's Sons, 1980), 10–11.

7. Kirk, "Is Adoption Second-Best?"

8. Kirk, "Is Adoption Second-Best?"

9. James, *Innocent Blood*, 39.

10. Bartholet, *Family Bonds*, 167.

11. Moore, *Adopted for Life*, 191.

12. Dietrich Bonhoeffer, "What Is Meant by 'Telling the Truth'?," in *Ethics* (New York: Macmillan, 1955), 363–72.

13. Bonhoeffer, "What Is Meant by 'Telling the Truth'?," 367–68.

14. Bonhoeffer, "What Is Meant by 'Telling the Truth'?," 366.

15. Bartholet, *Family Bonds*, 57–61.

16. Pertman, *Adoption Nations*, 87.

17. See the data provided by the Pew Research Center in Gretchen Livingston, "Fewer Than Half of U.S. Kids Today Live in a 'Traditional' Family," December 22, 2014, http://www.pewresearch.org/. Another 15 percent of children live with two parents who are in a remarriage.

18. Brent Waters, *The Family in Christian Social and Political Thought* (Oxford: Oxford University Press, 2007), 217.

19. Rob Palkovitz, "Gendered Parenting's Implications for Children's Well-Being," in *Gender and Parenthood: Biological and Social Scientific Perspectives*, ed. W. Bradford Wilcox and Kathleen Kovner Kline (New York: Columbia University Press, 2013), 215.

20. Palkovitz, "Gendered Parenting's Implications," 236.

21. Timothy P. Jackson, "Suffering the Suffering Children: Christianity and the Rights and Wrongs of Adoption," in Jackson, *Morality of Adoption*, 202. Jackson's normative position is qualified, however, by his belief that what he calls a "sanctity right" of needy children to be adopted (197–98) overrides other considerations, including a hesitation to place children for adoption with same-sex couples.

22. For my own view, see Gilbert Meilaender, "The First of Institutions," *Pro Ecclesia* 4 (Fall 1997): 444–55.

23. Joseph R. LaPlante, "Tough Times for Catholic Adoption Agencies," *OSV Newsweekly*, May 7, 2014, Our Sunday Visitor, https://www.osv.com/.

24. Martha C. Nussbaum, "Patriotism and Cosmopolitanism," in *For Love of Country: Debating the Limits of Patriotism*, ed. Joshua Cohen (Boston: Beacon Press, 1996), 7.

25. Augustine, *City of God*, trans. Henry Bettenson (New York: Penguin, 1984),12.22.

26. Nussbaum, "Patriotism and Cosmopolitanism," 11.

27. John Seabrook, "The Last Babylift," *New Yorker*, May 10, 2010, http://www.newyorker.com/.

28. Richard M. Lee, "The Transracial Adoption Paradox: History, Research, and Counseling Implications of Cultural Socialization," *Counseling Psychologist* 31, no. 6 (November 2003): 714.

29. Seabrook, "Last Babylift."

30. Seabrook, "Last Babylift."

31. For an especially vigorous critical view, see Kathryn Joyce, *The Child Catchers: Rescue, Trafficking, and the New Gospel of Adoption* (New York: Public Affairs, 2013).

32. "Facts and Statistics," under "Why We Do It," Congressional Coalition on Adoption Institute, accessed June 4, 2015, http://ccainstitute.org/.

33. "Statistics," on the website of the Bureau of Consular Affairs, U. S. Department of State, accessed June 4, 2015, http://travel.state.gov/content/adoptionsabroad/en/about-us/statistics.html.

34. Nila Bala, "The Children in Families First Act: Overlooking International Law and the Best Interests of the Child," *Stanford Law Review*, April 18, 2014, http://www.stanfordlawreview.org/online/children-families-first-act-overlooking-international-law-and-best-interests-child.

35. Bartholet, *Family Bonds*, 142–43. Without denying that money can sometimes corrupt international adoptions, Bartholet also suggests

that some of the accusations of "trafficking" are overstated. "The stories sometimes involve claims that what is characterized as a bribe may have been paid to an official in a country in which small payments to officials are a part of how official business is traditionally done" (154).

36. For an assertion that the 1972 NABSW statement did not in principle oppose transracial adoption for children who would otherwise remain in institutions or foster homes, see J. Toni Oliver (vice president of the NABSW), "Adoptions Should Consider Black Children and Black Families," *New York Times*, last updated February 3, 2014, http://www.nytimes.com.

37. Armand Marie Leroi, "A Family Tree in Every Gene," *New York Times*, March 14, 2005, http://www.nytimes.com.

38. Paul Lauritzen, *Pursuing Parenthood: Ethical Issues in Assisted Reproduction* (Bloomington: Indiana University Press, 1993), 133.

CHAPTER 4. Assisted Reproduction and Adoption

1. Jackson, "Suffering the Suffering Children," 214.

2. Peters, *For the Love of Children*, 69.

3. John A. Robertson, *Children of Choice: Freedom and the New Reproductive Technologies* (Princeton, NJ: Princeton University Press, 1994), 143.

4. Robertson, *Children of Choice*, 143.

5. Robertson, *Children of Choice*, 144.

6. Sarah Franklin, "From Blood to Genes? Rethinking Consanguinity in the Context of Geneticization," in *Blood and Kinship: Matter for Metaphor from Ancient Rome to the Present*, ed. Christopher H. Johnson, Bernhard Jussen, David Warren Sabean, and Simon Teuscher (New York: Berghahn Books, 2013), 292.

7. Kaja Finkler, *Experiencing the New Genetics: Family and Kinship on the Medical Frontier* (Philadelphia: University of Pennsylvania Press, 2000), 43.

8. Finkler, *Experiencing the New Genetics*, 120.

9. Finkler, *Experiencing the New Genetics*, 9.

10. Finkler, *Experiencing the New Genetics*, 136.

11. Gerard V. Bradley, "The Family Matrix," *Public Discourse*, May 7, 2014, http://www.thepublicdiscourse.com.

12. Bradley, "Family Matrix."

13. Bradley, "Family Matrix."

14. Bradley, "Family Matrix."

15. Jeanne Stevenson-Moessner, *The Spirit of Adoption: At Home in God's Family* (Louisville: Westminster John Knox, 2003), 106.

16. Moore, *Adopted for Life*, 106.

17. Moore, *Adopted for Life*, 88.

18. We should not forget, of course, that those whom we call donors should often more accurately be called vendors.

19. Kirk, "Is Adoption Second-Best?"

20. Oliver O'Donovan, *Begotten or Made?* (Oxford: Clarendon Press, 1984), 37.

21. O'Donovan, *Begotten or Made?*, 37–38.

22. Congregation for the Doctrine of the Faith, *Donum Vitae: Instruction on Respect for Human Life in Its Origin and on the Dignity of Procreation*, 1987, http://www.vatican.va/roman_curia/congregations /cfaith/documents/rc_con_cfaith_doc_19870222_respect-for-human -life_en.html.

23. Banner, *Ethics of Everyday Life*, 56.

24. Banner, *Ethics of Everyday Life*, 56.

25. Banner, *Ethics of Everyday Life*, 57.

26. Banner, *Ethics of Everyday Life*, 61 and 57.

27. J. David Velleman, "Family History," *Philosophical Papers* 34 (November 2005): 357–78. Further citations will be given by page number within parentheses in the body of the text.

28. Of course, Velleman knows that any older human being who raises us will share a very large percentage of our DNA, but we can know that and still understand the point he makes.

29. Thomas Aquinas, *Summa Theologica*, suppl., q. 54, a. 3.

30. O'Donovan, *Begotten or Made?*, 38.

CHAPTER 5. Adopting Embryos

1. Tamar Lewis, "Industry's Growth Leads to Leftover Embryos, and Painful Choices," *New York Times*, June 17, 2015, http://www.ny times.com. Lewis estimates, in fact, that the number of frozen embryos could be as high as one million.

2. Congregation for the Doctrine of the Faith, "*Dignitas Personae*: Bioethical Questions and the Dignity of the Person," September 8, 2008, www.vatican.va.

3. Congregation for the Doctrine of the Faith, *Dignitas Personae*, no. 19. Italics in original. References to *Dignitas Personae* will be given in parentheses within the body of the text.

4. Reverend Tadeusz Pacholczyk, "On the Moral Objectionability of Human Embryo Adoption," in *The Ethics of Embryo Adoption and the Catholic Tradition*, ed. Sarah-Vaughan Brakman & Darlene Fozard Weaver (n.p.: Springer, 2007), 71.

5. Pacholczyk, "Moral Objectionability," 82. It is not clear to me how or whether this qualified endorsement of ectogenesis is compatible with the following passage from *Donum Vitae*, the Congregation for the Doctrine of the Faith's 1987 *Instruction on Respect for Human Life in Its Origin and on the Dignity of Procreation*: "Techniques of fertilization *in vitro* can open the way to other forms of biological and genetic manipulation of human embryos, such as attempts or plans for fertilization between human and animal gametes and the gestation of human embryos in the uterus of animals, or the hypothesis or project of constructing artificial uteruses for the human embryo. *These procedures are contrary to the human dignity proper to the embryo*" (I, 6; italics in original). Likewise, the 2008 instruction *Dignitas Personae* criticizes cryopreservation in part on the ground that "it deprives them [the frozen embryos] at least temporarily of maternal reception and gestation" (18). If such a temporary deprivation is wrong, how could one endorse ectogenesis?

6. A similar proposal is made by Fr. Nicanor Austriaco: "Instead of implanting their adopted embryo into his mother's womb, adoptive parents could pay for the cryopreservation necessary for the survival of their child until incubators capable of bringing him to term are invented." Rev. Nicanor Pier Giorgio Austriaco, O.P., "On the Catholic Vision of Conjugal Love and the Morality of Embryo Transfer," in *Human Embryo Adoption*, ed. Rev. Thomas V. Berg, L.C., and Edward J. Furton (Philadelphia: The National Catholic Bioethics Center / Thornwood, NY: The Westchester Institute for Ethics & the Human Person, 2006), 132–33.

7. The full sentence reads as follows: "In order to come to the aid of the many infertile couples who want to have children, adoption should be encouraged, promoted, and facilitated by appropriate legislation so that the many children who lack parents may receive a home that will contribute to their human development." In my view, this sentence actually gets things a little backward. Better would be a sentence something like the following: "In order that the many children who lack par-

ents may receive a home, adoption should be encouraged, thereby also aiding the many infertile couples who want to have children."

8. Darlene Fozard Weaver, "Embryo Adoption Theologically Considered: Bodies, Adoption, and the Common Good," in Brakman and Weaver, *Ethics of Embryo Adoption*, 147.

9. Cf. Berkman, "Virtuous Parenting and Orphaned Embryos," 19: "The procreative good is ordered to bringing about new life, whereas the choice the woman makes in embryo transfer is to nurture an already existing human life."

10. The passage cited is in Congregation for the Doctrine of the Faith, *Donum Vitae*, II, B, 4. We should note that, whereas the concern for the unity of the marriage bond might be understood to rule out only in vitro fertilization that uses *donated* gametes, this concern would also seem to rule out fertilization outside the womb even if the sperm and ova used are those of husband and wife.

11. Congregation for the Doctrine of the Faith, *Donum Vitae*, II, B, 3.

12. Berkman, "Virtuous Parenting and Orphaned Embryos," 28.

13. E. Christian Brugger, "A Defense by Analogy of Heterologous Embryo Transfer," in Furton and Berg, *Human Embryo Adoption*, 224.

14. See "National Institutes of Health Guidelines on Human Stem Cell Research," National Institutes of Health, U.S. Department of Health and Human Services, accessed March 7, 2016, http://stemcells .nih.gov/policy/pages/2009guidelines.aspx.

15. National Bioethics Advisory Commission, *Ethical Issues in Human Stem Cell Research* (Rockville, MD: National Bioethics Advisory Commission, 1999), https://bioethicsarchive.georgetown.edu/nbac/.

16. James H. Jones, *Bad Blood: The Tuskegee Syphilis Experiment* (New York: The Free Press, 1993), 94.

17. Robert Jay Lifton, *The Nazi Doctors* (New York: Basic Books, 1986), 295.

18. Hans Jonas, "Philosophical Reflections on Experimenting with Human Subjects," in *Philosophical Essays: From Ancient Creed to Technological Man* (Englewood Cliffs, NJ: Prentice-Hall, 1974), 127.

19. See, for example, the website of Nightlight Christian Adoptions, accessed March 7, 2016, https://www.nightlight.org/snowflakes-embryo-donation-adoption/.

20. See, for example, the work of the National Embryo Donation Center at https://www.embryodonation.org. The fact that this organization speaks of "donation" rather than "adoption" of embryos makes

clear that its motives are less mixed. Its focus is primarily on embryo donation as a way of overcoming infertility rather than a way of offering life to frozen embryos.

21. Matthew 25:40. Cf. John Berkman, "The Morality of Adopting Frozen Embryos in Light of *Donum Vitae*," *Studia Moralia* 40 (2002): 138.

22. Reinhold Niebuhr, *The Nature and Destiny of Man*, vol. 1, *Human Nature* (New York: Charles Scribner's Sons, 1964), 222.

23. Austin Farrer, *Love Almighty and Ills Unlimited* (Garden City, NY: Doubleday and Company, 1961), 166. See, in general, the book's appendix, "Imperfect Lives" (166–68).

24. Farrer, *Love Almighty*, 166.

Conclusion

1. L. M. Montgomery, *Anne of Green Gables* (New York: Grosset & Dunlap, 1968), 229. References will be given by page numbers in parentheses within the body of the text.

2. John Paul II, "Address of the Holy Father John Paul II to the Meeting of the Adoptive Families Organized by the Missionaries of Charity."

Index

GILBERT C. MEILAENDER is senior research professor at Valparaiso University and Paul Ramsey Fellow at the Notre Dame Center for Ethics and Culture.